Eliminating Mr. Wrong

Dameon Smith

ISBN: 0615808425
ISBN-13: 9780615808420
Library of Congress Control Number: 2013908436
CreateSpace Independent Publishing
Platform, North Charleston, South Carolina

This book is dedicated to everyone in my life (past and present) who has helped to make me the person I am today.

Table of Contents

Preface

By definition, Mr. Wrong is someone who is not right for you. Just because a man is *your* Mr. Wrong doesn't mean he is a bad person; however, he is still not *your* Mr. Right. Eliminating this person has nothing to do with soliciting the services of your local "wise guy." Though you might be thinking this is not a bad idea for your last Mr. Wrong, who wants to be on TV with her face covered and the feds shoving her head into a squad car?

This is about you knowing what and who you want in your life and a path to achieve this. Wouldn't it be great to meet the man of your dreams without sifting through all the dim-wits and half-wits posing as "The One"? Sure it would! What do you think the odds are of hitting a home run on your first swing? It does happen, but the odds are not good. Invariably most women do have to do some sifting, and therein lies the dilemma—how do you know during the sifting process when the right man for you has arrived? This is no easy feat and has cost many a woman sleepless nights.

The fact is that when seeking Mr. Right you only have to be correct once. All previous selections, though some might have been pleasant, have all been incorrect choices for one reason or another. Throughout our daily lives we make many choices by a process of elimination without even thinking about it. When selecting a partner, this same process can be used effectively as long as you know what your deal breakers are, among other things. If you know that lying, cheating, or disrespect are things you will not accept then these are deal breakers and can be used as a base to narrow the field of eligible suitors. As you might already know, it's not quite that simple.

Everyone is unique in their likes and dislikes. Telling you who *your* Mr. Right should be is not what we will cover within the confines of this book. We will instead concentrate on narrowing the field so the odds are stacked in your favor. After all, if you could go back in time and eliminate some of the timewasters you have encountered, you probably would. Granted, some experiences, although they may not have turned out the way you wanted them to, did serve their purpose because you learned from them. This book is a guide for the everyday woman and was written using the experiences conveyed to me by both men and women. There is no professional psycho-analysis here; just the lessons learned from the scores of people interviewed who were willing and gracious enough to share their experiences with me.

You probably already know what traits will create that spark within you. The fact is that men will pick up on these same traits and in a flash try to use this knowledge to their advantage in getting your attention. Some will intentionally try to lead you astray while others will genuinely try to court you with good intentions—you can't knock a man for trying. But even the guy with genuine intentions can be wrong for you. He just might not know it, and that is why *you should*. Unless you are gaining something from the encounter, why would you want to waste your time with someone who is knowingly wrong for you?

Chapter 1
Finding Miss Right

To make the process of finding "The One" easier, eliminating certain of your own behaviors and thought processes is the most logical starting point. Starting here makes sense because while you have no control over what others say or do, you do have control over what *you* say or do and thus how you react to the situations you are in.

If you like a guy and he treats you like an afterthought you can choose to either accept this treatment or not. If you do nothing but hope he will soon change his behavior, you have indeed made a decision by doing nothing. Even though you have not physically done or said anything, you have made the decision to allow him to continue mistreating you and to keep the situation in a way that only benefits him. You, however, do have the option of letting him know that the relationship is not working for you and needs to be adjusted or scrapped. This might be a tough call, but it must be done if you intend to have a say in your own relationship.

The problem many women run into is that they set out to change how this man treats them by changing who *they* are without holding *him* accountable. Most of the time, this means trying to prove to him that she is the one for him by spending money on him, fawning over him, or doing anything to please him. While this might seem like a noble thought—doing what it takes to keep her relationship—it is undoubtedly wrong since all it does is put her in the position of being a chaser. Furthermore, this behavior is reactionary and forces her to invest time and emotions in a situation that she has little or no control over at this point.

Women are a forgiving breed, and it is this continual act of forgiveness that a lot of men exploit in their relationships. This can lead to the woman trying to figure out what's wrong with her when the real problem is with her partner. Once a woman thinks she has found her long-term partner, she will try her best to keep the relationship afloat even when it's obvious her partner is not doing likewise. This act of singlehandedly trying to "make it work" does nothing but overstate the man's importance, which in turn increases his indifference to the relationship. It is therefore not wise to try saving a relationship if you are the only one trying. You both must want it to work and both must be trying to make it work, not just talking about it. Many a time a woman's effort to keep the relationship intact is driven by the fact that another woman is involved; this added situation only serves to artificially inflate the man's value.

A much better approach is to be in control of yourself and, by extension, your situation. By doing this from the beginning, you can correct any issues that may arise before they become integrated into the relationship. This then allows you to maintain control of how your life and relationship will move forward.

That being said, it is easy to point fingers and blame others for our failures while we overlook our own glaring shortcomings. Before you take on the task of finding the right man for you, you need to:

I)Know who *YOU* are
II)Love yourself
III)Know your self-worth
IV)Know what you want
V)Embrace your inner strength
VI)Get a life

If you have already accomplished all of the above, you are ahead of the game. Don't skip ahead, however, as you just might learn something.

I)Know Thyself

Who are you? Are you the type of person who needs to feel wanted? Needs approval? Must be the center of attention? Must win all debates? Must have the last word? Avoids all confrontations?

Whatever your description of yourself turns out to be, you must decide whether you like or dislike who you are. Hopefully you like who you are as is, but even if you see room for needed change, that's good too.

While others can see your physical makeup, your mental and emotional states are left to only those who know you well. Even then, only you know the pain and anguish you might go through after certain experiences. If you truthfully feel you need to shore up your mental or emotional prowess then do whatever it takes to do so as these are key factors in achieving a stronger, better you.

Why do other women want you to listen and not respond? How many times has a girlfriend come to you needing to talk but not wanting you to respond? All she needs is a listening ear so she can get whatever is bothering her off her chest. The only reason she even needs someone to listen to her is because her emotional cup runneth over. At this point, she wants to be comforted more than she wants to hear your solution. This is why a guy who listens or pretends to listen will always get a woman's attention.

Sure, it's good to get things off your chest, and it's even better if, after you do, you don't continue on the same old path. You have to learn from your mistakes. Quite a few women get into a continual cycle of letting their emotions dictate their behavior. Even after repeated failure, this behavior of leading with emotions is quite common among women. To be honest, nothing compares to a good emotional rush. However, one definition of craziness is said to be "doing the same thing over and again but expecting different results." If your current way of doing things has not been working for you, you obviously need to modify your approach for better results.

If a guy opens up to you it's usually because he wants a solution so he can move on. In most instances, a woman who opens up to you just wants an emotional release. It's just the way it is. Most women are more in tune with their emotional being than most men. This would seem like an easier path to happiness for women, but because of the inability to control these same emotions in relationships, many women end up confused and conflicted. This, however, doesn't have to be the case.

Start by getting to know yourself. What really makes you happy? What are your weaknesses? Are you too trusting? Do you depend on others to make you happy? Do an honest self-evaluation. "Finding" yourself is the start of a great relationship with someone who cares about you... you. Emotional control, believing in yourself, and trusting your own judgment are all things that will strengthen once you find yourself. Knowing yourself will bring a level of happiness in your life.

Being happy is first and foremost in our existence. You must find your own happiness before you can promise to make others happy. What good is trying to make those around you happy if you are not happy? What value do you place on your own existence if your own happiness does not count?

You will have an inner peace once you reach a state of happiness, and this will then allow you to assist in making others happy. This happiness must come from within so it cannot be influenced by outside forces. Upon figuring this out, you will realize how insignificant many things that you once worried about have now become. You will be better able to put things in perspective and move forward because it is not worth losing your happiness over.

In finding this state of happiness, you will understand the importance of not allowing *anyone* to take this peace of mind away from you. No one has the right to make you unhappy but in pursuing their own happiness, others will not necessarily care about yours—that is left to you. If you choose to invite someone into your life, it's up to you to maintain your own happiness throughout the encounter. Protecting your happy state of mind is the base of any relationship, whether with family members, associates, or a mate.

Don't forget that your personal happiness is the ultimate goal here, so you must be happy with the complete package—physical, mental, and emotional. How can you attract the right person if *you* don't think you are attractive in all aspects? Once you are truly happy with you—the complete package—your self-confidence will skyrocket and others will feed off that. In addition, once you get to know yourself, it will be easier for you to guide others in how to get to know you.

II) First Love

First love is love of self, and it is a must. Without this self-love, you're in for a rough ride. First love allows you to have a deeper sense of self, thereby not allowing you to accept being treated as less than others.

In addition to loving your mental state, you need to love your physical being the way it is. Whether you have a crooked nose or crossed eyes, are a little fat, have a lot of fat, or need some fat or toning, whatever. If you want to make changes, that's great, as long as it's for you and not what someone else thinks you should do—health reasons aside.

If you think nose/eye surgery or weight loss/gain will help you love yourself, go for it. Just know that you should love yourself the way you are now and that anything else will just be an enhancement. How you perceive yourself does translate to others. Some people might be taken aback initially upon seeing something out of the "norm" but will quickly get over that initial response if you proceed as if all's well. Never apologize for other people's ignorance. If they have an issue with who you are, then that's their problem, not yours. If you do love yourself, you will understand this concept fully.

If you don't love yourself, you will not feel worthy of being loved by others. You might show this "I'm not worthy" behavior by always wanting to pay when you go out, putting yourself down, refusing compliments, gifts, etc. If someone gives you a compliment about how beautiful you look and your response is, "Thanks but I need to lose a little weight," your self-love obviously needs some work. Not loving yourself will leave you accepting whatever others feel you are worth even if you are being shortchanged. Loving yourself sets the standard by which you allow others to love you. If they fall short of your standards, your internal alarms will start going off. You will then request that they make the necessary adjustments to maintain the standard or eliminate them from your life. Be aware, however, that no one is *obligated* to love you, except you.

Self-love must not be confused with being conceited. Don't get caught up with yourself; maintaining balance is one of the keys to living a fulfilling life. Many aspects of life require some form of moderation. This, however, is not to say you should live a conservative or boring life, unless this is the way you want to. Live life to the fullest and enjoy all it has to give, but know when you are getting close to the edge.

If you choose to live on the edge, that's fine—just know where *your* edge is located. For example: *If you know that when you drink too much alcohol you get loud and rude— which could lead to fights—or that you get amorous—which could lead to one-night stands—regulate what you drink when you go out. By doing this, you will minimize living with regrets.*

An added benefit of self-love is self-confidence. Attacking your self-confidence is the starting point of some men's approach, and it works! You know the guy: He's the one who makes the snide remark or back-handed compliment about your perfume, your dress, or anything that might have you questioning yourself. The remark might be in the form of a joke to make you laugh at yourself, but nonetheless it's a ploy that puts doubt in your mind. It works because women are used to direct compliments and get intrigued by someone bold enough to be different. A woman will respond if only to convince the man that she is up to the challenge of his bold approach—game on. The tit-for-tat that follows can lead to emotional peaks, which is what a man wants, so be sure you know this game before you are all in. Could this be the man of your dreams? Sure, but if his focus is to convert the emotional chips he has just won from you into a ride on the wild side, keep him moving. If he is the right one—let him prove it!

III)Know Your Self-Worth

Your self-worth is what you think of yourself regardless of whose company you are in at any moment in time. This is a belief in yourself as a person and the knowledge that no one is more important than you are regardless of social status. You must elevate this belief in yourself if you are to succeed in any relationship, whether business or personal.

People tend to look at themselves through the eyes of the society in which they live. This cultural perspective is spearheaded by marketers and advertising campaigns telling you that to be cool your clothes must look like this, or your phone must be this brand, or the car you drive must be this or that make. You must be your own person and view yourself through your own eyes.

Knowing your self-worth is extremely important when dealing with others. Driving a new Mercedes might make you feel special, but it has nothing to do with your self-worth. What happens when it is parked and you are indoors? Will you be like the guy who talks about nothing except the things he owns?

It is not good enough to know your self-worth. You have to let others know that *you* know your self-worth and thereby show that you have self-esteem. If others know that you value yourself as a person, it will help to eliminate those time wasters who are just "window shoppers."

There are many men out there who are just "window shopping." These guys go after the path of least resistance hoping for an easy score. They will keep throwing their nets over and over hoping to catch an unsuspecting woman who is actively seeking a relationship.

These women make easy targets because most are so intent on finding a man that they get carried away on any emotional tide that rolls in. These women are usually starving for emotional interaction and jump at any chance offered to them because "a man hasn't made me feel like this in a long time." By focusing on the emotions and not the person, a woman in this state of mind tends to unknowingly shut down her natural defenses to keep the emotions flowing, thus making herself an easy target. All this is by design but can be avoided.

These "window shoppers" definitely don't want to waste their time with someone who has high self-esteem and knows what she wants. By letting your self-esteem shine through, you will eliminate these time wasters off the bat. Conversely, the self-assurance you will emit by letting your self-esteem shine through will attract men who are attracted to confident women. Among these men will be both the genuine and the players, but at least you won't have the other timewasters blocking the path of someone who might have genuine intentions.

A man must know that you have enough self-worth to leave the relationship if he acts the fool. His knowing this will give him pause before he commits to spur-of-the-moment decisions that lead to shenanigans. If a man knows that he won't be able to convince you to forgive him for his infidelity or disrespect, he is more likely to place value on the relationship. It is the value he has now placed on the relationship that will minimize the chances of him creeping or blatantly disrespecting you—basically it's not worth losing his relationship over.

If he says he loves you, you must see sacrifices being made to prove this—and not just spending money on you. It doesn't have to be major to begin with, but he must show he's willing to put you first on occasions. He might give a million and one excuses why he couldn't do this or that or he might say he's not into that type of thing. *Think about this: How many times have you seen a man treat his wife/girlfriend like dirt but turn around and bend over backward for a woman who treats him like dirt? This goes to show that **people will make the sacrifices for whomever they deem worthy.*** A man will do whatever he wants to do—justification allows this, as he can justify anything he chooses to do. Don't make excuses for him. If he thinks you are worth it, he *will* make the sacrifice for you.

Some women are so desperate to hear what they want to hear that instead of taking a man at his word, they instead supply an answer to explain what he meant. For example, if after dating for a few months you introduce him to others and he says "we are just friends," don't proceed to explain that he was just trying to be funny—*that's how he feels!* If you have to explain what he means every time he embarrasses you, you need to be honest with yourself and realize this can't be the man for you.

If you think you can make him change over time, you are sadly mistaken. If he's not willing to do the right thing when the relationship is new and hopped up on emotions, what are the chances he will make any sacrifice after the emotions have waned? An issue for many women is that a man who does not want to make any sacrifices can seem like a challenge. This perceived challenge intrigues us as humans—let the chase begin, because this is exactly what will happen if you fall for this. It will be the start of the old switcheroo where the woman ends up chasing the man then wonders when she became the chaser instead of the "chasee." Guys know this game well and some play it to perfection at the expense of a woman's emotional wellbeing. That being said, you have no one to blame but yourself.

You have to take ownership of your own emotional health. This takes a lot of strength, as we all like the fuzzy feeling we get from a good emotional rush. To ask you to turn off that sweet flow of emotion and brace yourself for the burning that will surely replace it should you have to walk away from a bad situation will definitely have you crying "foul." However, we have all seen the remnants of unmetered emotions run amuck: from destruction of property (keyed cars, broken windshields, or bleached clothes, etc.) to stalking, restraining orders, and, unfortunately, death. *Your emotional wellbeing is not something you should place in someone else's care.*

Too often women allow men to take absolute control of a relationship, thus controlling their emotions. If the relationship doesn't work, their first response is to start begging to work on the relationship. If that doesn't work, these women then go off the deep end, and getting even is the only thing on their mind. Avoid these self-destructive behaviors by embracing your self-worth.

There is no getting around finding and getting to know your self-worth if you want a strong, well-balanced emotional persona and thus a strong, healthy relationship. You cannot live in denial, blame others, or run from your inner issues because wherever you go...there you are. You have to own and address whatever issues you have. It is best to address your known issues *before* you bring someone else into your life.

IV)Know What You Want

Are you looking for Mr. Right or Mr. Right Now? Are you sure you want what you say you want? A sensitive man, a take-charge man, or an easygoing man? You must know what it is you want in a relationship. If you don't know, try to figure this out before going into a relationship. If you try to figure out what you want while you are in the relationship, you are now at the mercy of your emotions, and this is not good. Trying to figure it out "on the fly" can end up making you confused and second guessing yourself as to whether this is the right situation for you or not.

Know what you want going in, otherwise you could end up falling for anything that makes you feel good.

Some women have said they want a man who opens up and shares his innermost feelings—how she makes him feel and what she means to him, etc. This is of course in line with the woman's emotional wellbeing and an attempt to find out where the man's head is.

Don't, however, take all that is said at face value and be quick to jump at anything that vaguely resembles male sensitivity. If male sensitivity is what gets your emotions going, be careful how you proceed because players know how to play this game. If it's sensitivity you want, it's sensitivity you'll get. These guys will lie or imply to move things to the next level. You must know what you want without seeming desperate and obvious about it. Know how to maneuver yourself within a conversation to get the information you need.

If you think being upfront and direct is the best remedy for these situations at the beginning of a relationship, think again. Being direct too soon takes away the intrigue and has the guy wondering "what's your rush?" It makes him feel as if he's being interviewed for a job and therefore thinks you have an ulterior motive of trapping him.

If you know how you want a meal to taste, you can manipulate the ingredients to get the end result you want. However, how can you eliminate an ingredient from a recipe if you don't know how you want the final dish to taste? Once the cooking is done, you'll know if the ingredients, quantity, and quality were right or wrong, but by then it's too late.

You must know what you want from your partner (ingredients and quantity) and how you want your relationship to be (quality). You of course will be the mixer who brings it all together. Once you know how, you can steer the relationship in the direction you want as long as it's mutually agreed upon with your partner.

All this is not to say you should be sizing up a guy's finger for a wedding ring on the first date; rather, you should be sizing up where you are at this stage in your life. Maybe you truly don't want a relationship right now, and that is fine as long as you know this. Even though you may need to be calculating at times, all of us end up taking chances, but it is best to take that chance only after you have decided you can handle the consequences should your plans not go the way you hoped. Many a nervous breakdown has been the end result of not being able to handle the aftermath of a bad decision.

Before you invite someone into your life, be sure YOU are ready for the commitment and all that goes along with it. You could end up eliminating Mr. Right if you've been the problem all along. You might actually meet the right person, but if you're not ready that person will not get to meet the real you and you both will be cheated out of what might have been. This situation happens all the time. Not being ready could be caused by many different things, such as not knowing exactly what you want, toting emotional baggage through a door that has just been opened and not being aware of it, not ready for compromise, etc.

Do not give anyone the impression that they will be coming into the relationship to run your life unless this is what you want, at which point I suggest you re-evaluate your self-worth. You cannot, however, assume others will want a mutually run relationship, so things like this must be discussed even if it feels uncomfortable. Once you are at the point where you are ready to discuss the status of the relationship, you must let your partner know what it is you expect from him and what he should expect from you. This doesn't mean it will be an easily agreed upon arrangement. However, with mutual respect and compromise, most disagreements can be ironed out if you both think it's worth it and both want it to work.

V) Strength of a Woman

Women have great inner strength. The rock of so many families is the woman in the background who exhibits dogged determination and steadfastness in the face of imminent failure and doubt only to arise victorious. Much of this emotional heavy lifting goes unnoticed by "outsiders" but is celebrated by inner family members who know that these women(whether mother, grandmother, great-grandmother, or aunt) are the glue that keeps their family unit together.

Women's history of inner strength is such a well-kept secret because, unlike most men, women are usually not drawn to the bravado of announcing their accomplishments from the highest mountaintop. Because it is not publicized, both men and women tend to take a woman's inner strength for granted.

It is no surprise then why some women are so quick to sacrifice who they are for emotional utopia. They are enamored with the idea of playing the damsel in distress role where Prince Charming swoops in and saves her from the dragons of the world. This would be so sweet if only it were true. Wake up and understand that more often than not the dragon's best disguise is that tired, dusty old Prince Charming costume he has hanging in his closet. This he dons at the first sounds of a damsel in distress, so don't be so quick to discard your inner strength and make yourself a victim.

Downplaying your independence and inner strength or hiding your intellect so as not to turn off a man is cheating yourself. It is much harder to keep up the charade of being a person you are not than just being yourself. How long are you willing to be someone other than yourself, and at what cost? What happens when the "real you" surfaces? Even the man who is genuinely interested in you will start doubting the situation. Is he to believe that this new personality is the real you? That would mean that quite a bit of what has transpired might have been a lie. This puts you in the bad position of trying to convince him that you are who you say you are this time around. Don't risk wasting your own time; be yourself from the start!

If a woman knows the operation of a car's systems and takes it to a mechanic for a tune-up, should she play dumb because she likes the mechanic and doesn't want to risk hurting his feelings and losing him? If she chooses this route and it works for her (she gets her man), she had better plan on babying him on the other insecurities he will most likely have if he wasn't able to handle such a situation to begin with. It would be much better for her to show her knowledge and hope he is secure enough to engage her discussion on a higher level. The man for you has to be secure about himself whenever he's around you.

The easiest way to live and achieve happiness is to be yourself and do what you love. It becomes hard when you live your life to please others since your happiness now depends on validation from someone else.

Don't hide who you are by pretending to be the perfect woman. Have your basic ideals ready for him to see. These basic ideals will be the foundation on which you will start any relationship. If you offer a man a clean sheet in an attempt to look like the perfect woman for him, he will either try to mold you to his liking or hold this "perfect woman" against you.

The molding of a female is often seen in younger women who are dominated by older men because these women are not mentally mature enough to understand the ramifications of such behavior. If you pretend to be the "perfect woman," you leave yourself no room to be "normal," and the minute you falter, it will be used against you. To avoid these pitfalls, don't wait for anyone to validate you— be yourself and those who like you will do so knowing this is indeed who you are.

If you want people to see who you are then you must *be who you are.* Don't put up a front just to attract or impress a man. You won't be able to keep up this bogus persona, and he will eventually see through it and then brand you as a fraud. He will then use his newly created ideas about you as justification to play games and string you along. In his mind, you are a fraud anyway, so who are you to judge him and his antics? Don't expect a man to confront you if he thinks you are pretentious; all you've done is given him an excuse to act the fool until he's ready to move on.

Dameon Smith

During an interview, a young lady told me she stood open-mouthed and dumbfounded when her partner started listing what he considered her pretentious behavior. He had used his idea of her as his reason to keep looking even after the relationship was well over a year old. Avoid the games that follow a false personality by being yourself.

You can be yourself forever; that is not a problem. The problem is trying to still be yourself around someone who makes you giddy and appeals to you on different levels, meaning: your emotions can get in the way. When you are around such a person, your internal bells are going off, signaling that this could be "The One." The other half of this equation that you can't forget is that *you* must also appeal to him in the same way. You must be strong enough to calm your emotions and allow him to show you that you do appeal to him.

Don't be scared to show your inner strength. If you intimidate a man by just being yourself, can this really be the man for you? The right man will appreciate and love you for who you are even if you are perceived as a challenge. As a matter of fact, being perceived as a challenge will work in your favor if you are not obnoxious about it. Most men are usually up for a good challenge and this will allow you to see *his* emotional side.

A man exposing his emotional side (good or bad) can give you a better understanding of who he is and thus allow you to better identify whether his intentions are good or bad.

VI) Get a Life

"Get a life!" We have all used this saying in jest or have had someone jokingly say it to us. But seriously—*get a life*!

By having "a life," you are less likely to lose yourself in a newly forming relationship or in an already established one. Getting "a life" minimizes insecurity, which will have you hanging on to his last words. If he says "I'll call you *later*," insecurity will make you upset if he calls the next day. Get a life so you are not sitting around waiting for "*later*" to come.

Doing things outside of a work or home environment that stimulates you has many benefits. It allows you to get away from the daily grind and do something that is only done to make you happy. It allows you to blow off steam, relieve stress, and free your mind.

Nothing else matters but your peace of mind. This part of your life is critical in maintaining the needed balance you must have to properly deal with this seesaw world we live in. There are always many different things vying for your attention, wanting to pull you this way or that way. All this stirs emotions both good and bad that can take you up or down. Having "a life" is "me time" that will help you stay grounded; it is what you do to get away from the outside world.

Whatever you choose to do in freeing your mind—whether it be hanging with girlfriends, choir practice, or weekend sports, etc.—it must add value to your life in order for it to serve its purpose. If it does, you will protect its existence because you know its importance in helping to maintain your sanity and in creating an emotional outlet.

If you have "a life" and meet someone you like, you will be better equipped to deal with this new emotional situation. By maintaining your life, you will keep this new situation in perspective, thereby not finding yourself over-run with emotions. Your even-keeled approach will give you the sense that you are in control of your life, and this in itself tends to attract other curious humans who will wonder "what is it about her?" It's about you not letting this new emotional situation disrupt your life and choosing instead to take control of how your life will be lived. Men are intrigued by this.

If you are already in a relationship, by having a life you allow yourself and your partner room to breathe. This takes stress off the relationship since there is no feeling of obligation involved. Each person is allowed time to do things outside the relationship that keeps him or her happy. A man in this type of relationship doesn't get the feeling of being trapped and is always intrigued by your independence and ability to be happy even without him no matter how long you have been together. Not being too available for a man also gives him something to think about. Most men understand the value of having "a life"; this is proven by all the extracurricular things most men do, such as playing card games, participating in sports, watching sports, restoring a car, etc.

Conversely, a man who does not want you to have a life that does not include him in every aspect is an insecure person and is trouble looking for a place to happen. This is your future control freak/stalker and must be eliminated.

Chapter 2

Mr. Wrong

❧❦

Identifying Mr. Wrong can be obvious or quite complex due to mitigating circumstances.

On the obvious side, if a man does nothing to get your emotional gears turning after spending the requisite time around you, you need to walk away from the situation. If you choose to proceed, you will likely end up with buyer's remorse. We have all had that ill feeling of buyer's remorse. Deep down you felt uneasy about the transaction but did it anyway only to regret it later. Your emotional wellbeing is too precious to let it become the victim of buyer's remorse. Too often a woman will stare at an obviously bad situation and jump right in because desperation gets the best of her.

Mitigating circumstances such as societal pressures (not married by a certain age), internal pressures (getting older and no kids), and insecurities (need to feel wanted) are but a few of the many circumstances that can make identifying Mr. Wrong quite complex. People living in the moment can be oblivious to signs that are otherwise obvious to others around them because of these circumstances. Identifying Mr. Wrong becomes even harder when you add the fact that once emotions get involved, judgment becomes even more impaired.

Dameon Smith

There are two types of Mr. Wrong: Good Mr. Wrong and Bad Mr. Wrong. Regardless of whether they are good or bad, understand that they are *both wrong* for you.

I)Good Mr. Wrong

Good Mr. Wrong is not necessarily a bad person; he's just not right for *you*. He will come in different guises. He might be a longtime friend, a friend of the family, a co-worker, or a total stranger who has genuine interest in pursuing a long-term relationship with you. He will be doing and saying all the "nice" things because he genuinely likes you. As you know so well, just because a man genuinely likes you does not mean you should start a relationship with him. You have to feel the same, otherwise you will experience buyer's remorse sooner or later.

Good Mr. Wrong is usually easily spotted by a woman's super sensitive "Mr. Wrong" radar. This radar turns on the lights and sounds the alarm so there is no chance of him sneaking into this woman's life. She can confidently let this man advance to the next level if she wants to investigate further should her curiosity be piqued. All this is possible because she has been forewarned by her "Mr. Wrong" radar, and this man is now under full surveillance.

Good Mr. Wrong is usually not an issue for most women. You see him coming a mile away and have the bright lights on him the whole time. An example of this is the "nice" guy who makes himself too available, buys you things, will do anything you want when you want but does nothing for you emotionally. You have this guy wrapped around your little finger and know exactly how to play him. Whether you choose to string him along or let him down easy (so as not to hurt his feelings), you have him covered. You have this situation under control because there is very little movement on the emotional scale, so you are in full control of your emotions and therefore can make rational decisions.

The ironic thing is that this very guy might be a "dog" to other women but is like a puppy to you. That is just a part of the circle of life. Nonetheless, he's still wrong for you if he doesn't bring that joy to your insides.

Some women who meet this good Mr. Wrong will try to make the relationship work because, after all, he does like her, and if she could just find a way to like him as more than a "friend," she would have a workable arrangement. With this new project of "trying to like him" in mind and knowing that "settling for" can be a miserable existence, she proceeds to try to "fix" him. She knows she is choosing to gamble against her better judgment, but the possibilities her mind has created are enough for her to give it a try. Word to the wise—if you have to "fix" him to like him, it's unlikely he's the one.

This man is the perfect match for someone...just not for you. The odds of making such a situation work is not much better than trying to date a gay friend—there's no emotional spark. Furthermore, you usually run into major problems when you do meet someone who gets you going emotionally. You end up in a committed relationship but now you are emotionally attracted to someone else.

Another example of Good Mr. Wrong is the guy who starts out with good intentions then later realizes you are not the one for him and tells you so. Once he tells you it's not going to work, be appreciative that he is being forthright with you. Grit your teeth, swallow your pride, temper your emotions, and allow him to move on.

If you try to convince him to stay and you succeed at doing this, you may have just turned a prince into a frog or a Good Mr. Wrong into a Bad Mr. Wrong. You have now given him the ultimate power to control the relationship. If a man tells you it's not going to work, you better believe him—*it's not going to work!* Don't try to tell him you were meant for each other or that you both can work it out. He knows whether he wants to be with you or not. You might convince him to stick around, but you are only delaying the inevitable. If he sticks around, it's just until the next best shows up and then he's either gone or he'll have you chasing your tail trying to keep up with him. Either way, you will be left picking up the pieces and regretting the day you convinced him to stay. Ask a friend who's been through it.

Don't waste your time. If he wants to go, let him go. If he stays and starts using you, you have no one to blame but yourself. Don't let a good man go bad. Let him go; otherwise you might be introducing him to a player lifestyle that he ends up liking, thus making it harder for the next woman.

II)Bad Mr. Wrong aka The Player

Much like Good Mr. Wrong, Bad Mr. Wrong will say some nice things, but in addition he will also say the "right" things. These "right things" are what will get your emotional train on track, and from that point on his main goal will be to get those emotions rolling like a runaway locomotive.

There are two types of players, the upfront and the covert. The upfront player is the guy who lets you know from the start that he doesn't want a relationship. You cannot hold this guy responsible for any emotional damage that you may incur if you know going into the relationship that he's just "having fun." If you agree to this arrangement you cannot later try to change the wording of the agreement or bring your feelings into the fray.

If you are not sure about the fine print of such an agreement, have your girlfriend/lawyer give it the once over and your girlfriend/psychiatrist on standby should your emotions betray you and you start having feelings for this guy. The standard sentence in this situation before the crying begins is, "Look, you knew the deal before you got in." I'm sure you've heard it. It might not have been said to you, but you have heard it. Your best bet is to not get involved if you know you can't handle such a situation. Most women have no problem in this situation because, as stated, they know the deal going in.

The covert player ("The Chameleon") is the true purpose of this book. Unlike the upfront player, The Chameleon does not make his intentions known. His sole purpose is to be deceitful and give the impression that he's The One. His mission won't be complete until he gets what he wants, whether it's sex, financial support, emotional support, or just having his ego stroked after another conquest before he moves on. He will be moving on when your time is up and he knows this going in. How the relationship ends might be orchestrated or incidental, but it will only end when he wants it to end if you allow him to play his game.

The Chameleon is adept at finding a woman's weaknesses and being the crutch for that weakness, thus encouraging her dependency and faith in him. If for example he realizes that you are scared of being alone or are desperately looking for a long-term relationship, he will slowly start to supply the necessary pieces needed so you can paint a picture in your head of how comforting such a relationship with him would be. He might start discussing hardcore future plans if he thinks this won't set off an alarm. Hinting at the future and allowing you to create your own future paradise is also a viable option as this puts the blame squarely on you for reading into the things he says. "Looking into a cruise for us" implies future bonding, but "looking into" doesn't mean you will be going anywhere.

The difficulty women have in dealing with The Chameleon is that it can take months, even years, to uncover the fact that this guy was a player all along. His ability to blend in with friends and family members provides the perfect guise to deceive. He will play this deceitful role to perfection until he has had his fill and it's time to move on or until he has been exposed.

How then does a woman identify a Chameleon and thus eliminate him from her life? Or better yet, how does she identify him *before* he gets into her life?

Let's start with the fact that only those able to connect with you emotionally will make your list. This still leaves quite a bit of room for The Chameleon to work since creating emotional spark is one of his best attributes. After the emotions are covered, women eliminate men using different variables. Some eliminate by looks (face or body), financial status, or social standing, to name a few. Others go down a mental checklist trying to identify deal breakers.

Regardless of how this process is handled, the end result for all women is happiness. However, when asked what they want from a relationship, over 90 percent of the women interviewed responded along the lines of "a committed relationship that includes respect and someone who makes me happy." Therein lies an incorrect thought process when it comes to relationships. Though it might not seem obvious at first, looking for someone who "makes me happy" puts you in a dependent state of mind. If you do find someone who makes you happy, you will be depending on that person to *keep* you happy. This now gives him the power to determine your level and frequency of happiness. Is that what you want? A better thought process would be to find someone to share your happiness with. This puts you in the mindset to find your own happiness before you go looking for Mr. Right. Once you find your own happiness, this eliminates the dependency that Chameleons manipulate to advance their agenda.

Sometimes people invite others into their lives without analyzing the real reason they are doing this. It is easy to get carried away by emotions, but have you ever stopped to think why this person makes you feel this way? Why does this person get your emotions flowing? You need to know the answer to this before you make the move to start a relationship with this person.

As an example: *Many people will invite someone into their lives only because they assume others will think this person is attractive, rich, or a celebrity (even if only on a local level). Being the partner of this attractive/rich person makes them feel special, and it is this special feeling that gets their emotions going. Usually in this situation, the attractive/rich person can do no wrong because the woman needs him around to keep that special feeling present. It is only after many issues and drama that the woman realizes that this attractive person was never really a compatible match.*

Needless to say, this kind of behavior, which elevates the man's status within the relationship without merit, is the perfect situation for The Chameleon. A woman living off the looks or social status of her partner has absolutely no control over where this relationship goes. Because her happiness and self-worth depend on the presence of this person, she becomes a slave to maintaining the relationship. This is obviously not a situation you want to be in.

The selection process is where most relationships fail, so choose wisely.

Generally people want the best for themselves, but in selecting a partner many choose someone they think *others* will approve of "Her fiancé is rich," "Her boyfriend is handsome," or "Her man is a celebrity" means she has done well for herself. Many women choose this path instead of selecting someone who will be best in complimenting their life as a person. If your partner happens to be a rich, handsome celebrity and he enhances your life as a person, that's great. It doesn't help if, however, he's a rich, handsome celebrity who treats you like crap.

Though there are no concrete rules in dealing with men, there are some basic rules and common sense guidelines that do help and will eliminate most Chameleons. Allow emotional control, your self-worth, and situations to eliminate the rest.

Chapter 3
Rules / Guidelines

ॐॐ

"When the fool learns the rules, the game is over."
Know the rules and understand the guidelines.

There are exceptions to every rule. If you choose to gamble with your emotions and want to play the exception, that's OK, as long as you can handle the consequences should your gamble not payoff. The odds of an exception coming through are stacked against you, and furthermore, if you lose, the emotional damage will be more intense. It is more intense because along with the regular emotions involved with putting a relationship together, your emotions get amped up anticipating a victory at beating the odds (gambling does this).Gamblers get hooked on trying to land the big payoff and never stop trying until they are either destroyed or have an intervention.

Many women get caught up in a situation of high risk/low reward where they expend a lot of emotional energy trying to be with a man who could care less about being in a relationship with them. This situation is high risk because if the man isn't trying to be in a relationship, chances are he won't end up in one. The problem is that in trying to make something out of nothing, the woman is investing emotionally the whole time. In doing this she is gambling her emotional wellbeing on a situation that has very little chance of survival.

It is a low reward situation because even if she does convince him to be in a relationship with her, she will end up toting the full weight of this relationship because he could care less. It has been said and proven that *the person who cares the least about the outcome of a relationship gains the most from said relationship.* This of course is because the woman who wants to keep the relationship going ends up killing herself to make it work.

Being confident in who you are, not being the jealous type, and not being needy are but a few guidelines that have lasting effects on relationships. Depending on your personality, some of the guidelines below might need to be rules. A little jealousy, for example, can be expected, since after all we are only humans. If you, however, know that when you get jealous you lose control and all hell breaks loose with wild accusations and pocket searching, etc., you might want to make "not being the jealous type" a rule instead of a guideline. Somewhat like an alcoholic avoiding *any* form of alcohol or situations that could lead to a relapse.

I)Never Be a Chaser

What is your reason for chasing a man? Do you just want him to stop and see that you were meant to be? That you are good for each other if only he would give it a chance? Do you not think he's smart enough to know what he wants?

If you end up chasing a man, you will be doing the exact opposite of what you should be doing. In today's society, some women are all about being bold and initiating the first contact. There is absolutely nothing wrong with this depending on how it's done and what you choose as your follow-up step.

Eye contact, a smile, or basic body language is all an interested man needs so he knows that the next move is his. A courteous "hi, how are you?" or similar greeting should be your last move to generate interest. If you choose to jump into this man's space after doing the above, you have just diminished your self-worth and put yourself at a major disadvantage.

If he is interested in you, you will never have to go beyond a "first line." The moment you forge past the greeting stage into his space you have given him the power to decide if *you* are worthy. At this point you are now viewed as either easy, really into him, or aggressive. If he likes aggressive women, *ding ding*, you are in and your gamble has paid off. If on the other hand he thinks you are really into him, you leave yourself in the position of being taken for granted.

If you are mentally strong enough, a situation like this won't be an issue for you. Ideally, you will meet a man who is appreciative of a woman finding him interesting enough to boldly initiate the opening conversation. Unfortunately, there are men out there who are all about the game, and if your mental makeup is not up to par, you are starting off a few strokes back with a huge handicap.

Some men will just think you are being easy and will treat you as such. This is shown by the aggressive and dismissive behavior they exhibit when meeting a woman for the first time who initiated the contact. This kind of man has already judged you based on the situation or circumstance that brought you together. You definitely don't want to seem easy…unless you are up for a one- or two-night stand.

Unless you have mastered the "switcheroo," which subtly turns the "chasee" (the person being chased—in this case the man) into the chaser, you will lose on this gamble. You might get to hookup, but it won't be a long-term proposition for him.

If you chase after a man, the odds are that he most likely won't look at this situation as him being special but rather as you being easy. Should you chase after a man and catch a chameleon, you have no one to blame but yourself. Once you give a man the signals (smile, body language, first line) and he doesn't approach, keep it moving.

<u>Different Thought Process</u>: *Treat the guy you like with a touch of indifference, the same way you would treat the guy you are not attracted to, and you will get his attention—if* he likes you. *Have you ever noticed how the guy you are not attracted to never stops, no matter how you try to be subtle in turning him off? That's because he perceives you as a challenge. Don't be scared of turning off the guy you like because you are not all over him. If he is truly interested in you, this won't turn him off. If it does, he was never really interested in you. No man wants the woman of his dreams to be easy!*

II) You Can't Buy Love

Most women know you can't buy love. However, when they are doing it, they reclassify their behavior so they can justify doing so. If you are in a relationship and you are lending more money before getting repaid the last loan…you are paying your way. You might justify it by saying "He's going through tough times" or "He can't find a job he likes," but don't ante up for that second loan and see what happens.

If you are always the one shelling out the lion's share of all major and minor expenses…you are paying your way. You might justify it by saying "I don't mind paying," but the truth is if you don't, he won't, and now you have a dilemma, so it's easier just to pay.

If you are always showering him with gifts…you are paying your way. Your justification may be "He's my man and I love doing it." Well, are you not "his woman"? How come he doesn't do the same? Think self-worth.

These are just a few examples to show how some women will justify spending their hard-earned money on a man just to keep him. This is not to say a woman can't pay her own way or help if she can. Just know that if these types of behavior are the norm in your relationship, you are indeed paying to keep the relationship going.

The conscience of a guy who really means you well will kick in before the situation becomes habit forming to the point where you think you are doing all this spending out of love. His conscience won't allow him to take advantage of you. The Chameleon, however, will not stop you from spending and will be comforting, understanding, and humbled that you are indeed expressing your love for him by spending your hard-earned money on him.

Do you have the guts to say no and the courage to deal with the consequences that may follow? If not, you have some soul searching to do. If you don't think you are "paying your way," the next few times these situations pop up, just don't pay. This way you can see if you are right or wrong.

Different Thought Process: *Discuss financial compatibility before you take the relationship to the next level. Where you plan to be in the next few years and how you plan to get there, etc. This puts financial responsibility in the forefront and places a conscience on your spending. Financial compatibility is hardly discussed but is a very important part of every relationship and **must** be addressed.*

If for example his entrepreneurial endeavors will require financial backing and you are expected to be a source of funds but he refuses to consult a financial guru, be afraid...be very afraid.

If he has no problems with you spending your money loosely on him, what does this say about his regard for future plans? This just proves he's in it for "the now" and your future will be mired in bills created to keep him happy. Keep it moving.

III)Opposites Don't Attract

We have all heard that opposites attract. This may be true if you're a magnet but not so much when dealing with human personality, e.g. *If you are a giver, don't be with a taker.*

When was the last time you heard a conversation like this: "Hi, how are you? Do you believe in God?" "No, I'm an atheist." "Wow, really? I'm a Christian. I think we are meant for each other." Simplified but here's the point: Those that say opposites attract are usually taking a small sample of a much larger whole and trying to make that smaller sample the norm only because it fits whatever point they are currently trying to make.

Eliminating Mr. Wrong

Let's say John and Mary have a known, strong relationship. People might see Mary enjoying her Saturdays at the park bike riding, jogging, or picnicking while John is at home enjoying his Saturdays watching sports on TV. These are definitely opposite types of activities, and to the casual friend or observer, their relationship is strong yet they are opposite in their activities. Making the statement in this case that opposites attract would be incorrect. What the observer might fail to realize is that the strength of their similarities far outweigh the different preferences they may have in certain aspects of their life together. Out of public view, they may be bonded by a combination of quite a few things such as music, cooking together, talking for hours about nothing in particular, religion, or sex, to name a few.

These things are what will keep the relationship together in spite of the "opposites." The uninitiated will focus on the differences, thus trying to make factual points based on partial truths. Furthermore, the differences you might see as opposites in a strong relationship might be the time apart that the relationship needs to breathe, thereby creating a healthy balance within the relationship.

Since no two people are exactly alike, there will be differences. As long as you both agree that you can live with these differences without sacrificing who you are, it will all work out for the good. Some people believe that when two people come together to create a relationship, the two should become one to make the relationship stronger. Since this is currently physically impossible, the personality becomes the victim. Maintain your core identity; this is who your partner was attracted to in the first place. If your partner is trying to change who you are, then he is the wrong person.

I'm sure you have seen a friend, relative, or even yourself get into a relationship and totally change into someone barely recognizable to those around him or her. More than likely, the differences in this relationship outweigh the similarities, and this is why one person has to sacrifice to the point of being a totally different individual. These people are usually so afraid of losing what they have invested with the other person that they choose instead to sacrifice their own personality. The rationale is usually that they are doing it for the good of the relationship.

No relationship is worth losing the essence of who you are. The right man for you will respect your differences but embrace the similarities, thereby eliminating the need for you to change who you are in order for the relationship to work.

Needless to say, The Chameleon will tell you that you need to change if you want the relationship to work. This will make his goal of deceiving you for the long-term that much easier. His statement will create doubt, leaving you to second guess yourself and wondering if you do need to change who you are. At this stage it becomes very difficult to be objective in your assessment.

This is why it is better to do this self-evaluation *before* you bring someone into your life, thereby avoiding the possibility of emotions playing a part in your decision. If you already know who you are, you will be able to easily spot the man who is trying to pull the wool over your eyes as opposed to the man who truly sees a problem you need to address.

Different Thought Process: *No matter how good certain aspects of the relationship might be, if the differences outweigh the similarities, you must move on. If your mate is happy at home waiting for you but the thought of you going home to him makes you sigh, you obviously have opposing views of where the relationship is—his sanctuary cannot be your hell. Do not cling to the little good you see in him if the bad is obviously not worth it. The mothering part of you mixed with societal issues and a pinch of desperation might make you want to "fix" him, but you are much better off letting him go and moving on.*

IV) Never Believe Sex Talk
"He said he loved me."

Not believing sex talk might seem obvious. No one believes anything said during mid-stroke, right? Mostly true, but it can put doubt in the mind of a woman who is emotionally deficient. This causes her to wonder if he meant what he said or if it was just the heat of the moment. An emotional deficit will cause an otherwise well-balanced woman to fall prey to words or situations that strike an emotional chord.

This is where The Chameleon is at his best—preying on the emotionally starved. His words and the moments he creates are like manna from above, leaving you breathless yet fulfilled while making you float on air thinking nothing but blissful thoughts. However, before you take flight on this new, wonderful feeling, slow down and catch your breath. Just because you haven't felt like this in a long time doesn't mean you should throw caution to the wind and blindly jump in. Don't fall victim to emotional deficit; enjoy the moment but be careful as you move forward.

Anything said before, during, or after sex is classified as sex talk and should be disregarded as a by-product of the moment, especially if it involves the word "love."Some men will say whatever it takes to close the deal once things get past a certain point. Men are at their convincing best in the moments leading up to and during physical foreplay. What some women don't understand is that in most instances, foreplay of *the mind* i.e. mental stimulation, is where the game is won or lost. Many a time after the fact, a woman will lie there puzzled wondering *how the hell did that happen?* What she has failed to realize is that the mental orgasm she achieved earlier during the tit for tat mind game made the physical act a foregone conclusion.

"He told me he loved me." This is much like the "drunken man syndrome" where some people have to be drunk to say what's on their minds. Why did he wait until sex to say certain things? Don't fall for this and give him the easy way out. If he meant what was said during a sexual episode (before, during, or after) he should be able to repeat it without you asking if he meant what he said.

<u>Different Thought Process</u>: *Enjoy the moment but take it for what it is. Nothing said during sexual episodes (before, during, or after) should have value. Chameleons are great at heightening emotions, and sex talk is just one of many ways of doing so. Anything said must be followed by actions that demonstrate the sincerity of what was said.*

VI)Compromise is a Two-Way Street

No matter how much you have in common with someone, there will be some things that you disagree on. Since we don't live in a perfect world, disagreement is natural. As long as the issues causing the disagreement are not going against either of your core beliefs or standards you should be able to work it out with each other. This is assuming you and your partner are reasonable individuals.

Every disagreement must come to a mutually accept-able resolution; otherwise it will become a recurring issue that must be addressed each time it arises. If not addressed, it will start creating cracks that will shatter the relationship sooner or later. Every resolution, however, does not have to solve a problem—sometimes you have to agree to disagree.

Depending on what the issue is, it might not be worth the aggravation that a back and forth argument will create. Each person's agreeing to respect the other person's opinion while still believing in their own is sometimes the best solution to moving past this particular issue.

If, however, you are always the one giving in even though you truly believe you are correct, you need to re-evaluate your relationship. Are you giving in just to pacify him in order to keep the peace but complain to your girl-friends how dismissive he is of your opinions? If so, you need to re-evaluate your self-worth.

Chameleons are not into making compromises. They will not change who they are for a relationship they don't believe in. If a man refuses to compromise, he obviously doesn't think you are worth it. This doesn't mean he will never compromise, just not for you. People will ultimately do whatever they want if they think it's worth it for them to do so.

Different Thought Process: *If he refuses to compromise and takes a hard stance against most of the things you suggest, you are either not compatible or you have a chameleon on your hands. Either way…keep it moving.*

VI)If It's All About Your Body

If all of a guy's compliments toward you are about your looks even after a few dates or in your relationship, you better not gain weight or lose your tone. Or if he likes you plump, you better not lose weight.

Many women will start a long-term relationship knowing that the feature attraction for their partner is their looks. Years later, after Father Time comes calling and her body shape starts to change because of maturity, she wonders why the man is now making disparaging remarks. Who's to say how anyone's body will look as time passes? However, if your body at twenty-five is all he's interested in and you allow this, you are painting yourself into a corner. The fact is you cannot look twenty-five the rest of your life. If you allow a man to quantify you by your looks, you are allowing him to use an unfair means of judging you over-time. Unless you are among the very rare within the species blessed with killer genes or plan on plastic surgery to maintain that youthful look, you will be doomed to failure by his standards.

The irony of course is that most of the time the man telling the woman that she is gaining weight or losing her shape doesn't look so trim and fit himself. Not to mention the fact that he doesn't have to deal with childbirth or hormonal issues and all the stress they place on a woman's body. What if *you* are the attractive partner the other person needs in order to validate himself? If you know for sure that this is the way you will always look and this is the look he will always want, you can take your chances and see where that leads.

<u>Different Thought Process</u>: *The bottom line is not to allow anyone to judge you by your looks. Your looks can't be your only redeeming value. If so, your relationship will last only as long as your looks do or as long as he still likes that look. If a man insists on judging you this way, he doesn't respect you and he's letting you know he's a chameleon. Remember that a good relationship cannot last without mutual respect.*

VII)Ask The Tough Questions

The emotional boat ride is a pleasant, refreshing place to be. Floating out in the middle of nowhere blissfully thinking about nothing but the stars above and the relaxing sounds of the ocean gently playing the music of love to your ears while you sip from a half-full glass of your favorite brew…*Snap out of it!*

Know that before you venture on this emotional ride, you must ask and get the answers to the tough questions required to move the relationship from dockside into navigable waters. At dockside, everything is still under wraps in the relationship. No commitments have taken place, no major sacrifices have been made, etc. Save the emotional ride until the relationship has gone far enough where you can discuss plans and intentions. Once the relationship has left the dock, you are now committed to whatever ride different situations may provide.

Before you set sail in your new relationship, make sure you and your partner agree that this is a mutually exclusive relationship or that you are both free to keep dating. Few things aggravate a man more than finding out he has been

Dameon Smith

in a committed relationship that he knew nothing about. You must be on the same page here.

You cannot assume exclusivity because if left to their own vices, most men will want their cake and eat it too— The Chameleon can be a long-term presence in your life if allowed to have a "sidepiece" (a woman on the side). You must state your case and get a clear response in return. Make sure that if he agrees you will be exclusive, it's not just to take you off the market while he continues playing the field.

Asking the tough questions eliminates making assumptions and can save you from wasting your time. The nature of things such as his drinking problem or you burning one every now and then can lend themselves to direct observation. Other things might not be as obvious but must still be addressed. Discussing career goals (plan to relocate, etc.), religious beliefs (if any), financial status (how many outstanding loans to burden the relationship), kids, etc. are things that are not obvious but cannot be ignored if you are at the point of commitment. Any of these can be deal breakers, so you need to know before you commit.

Some women do not ask the tough questions because they already know that the answers are probably not what they want to hear, so they choose to live in blissful ignorance. Low self-esteem creates a fear of losing what they currently have, so they choose to continue investing time and emotions and settle for instant gratification. Feeling good now is used to suppress the knowledge of being used or of pending problems, and while you can fool others, it's much harder to fool yourself.

Eliminating Mr. Wrong

A young lady I spoke with told me of a time she wanted to talk to her boyfriend about their lack of quality time together. After putting her off for a few days, he finally agreed for her to come over to his place and talk about it. Upon her arrival at his place, the initial conversation was about past good times, which led to them having "great" sex. Once the sex was over, he begged to move the "real talk" to another day. According to her, she felt like crap on her "drive of shame" back home because she knew deep down that he was just using her.

Even though she wanted to discuss the state of the relationship, this young lady allowed the talk of good times to suppress what might otherwise have been a difficult discussion. By accepting the feeling of instant gratification, she saved herself the moments of anguish she suspected were imminent. The issue here is that she still went through moments of feeling down (on the drive home and after) and her problem still remained unresolved. By handling it the way she did, she also further damaged her self-esteem. If your partner does not enhance your self-esteem he could be destroying it.

He must respect the bond you have agreed upon whether or not rings and vows have been exchanged. You must make sure that the man in your life is not only investing time but is also emotionally invested in the relationship. Spending quality time together allows the strengthening of emotional bonds and helps to verify his commitment level regarding the relationship.

Quality time is not all about the activity but more about enjoying the company of the other person. It is about moments, not money. You can have a lousy time on an expensive trip and a great time at the park. You will remember both but only one of them fondly. Since quality time is about sharing good moments with someone else, you have to be open-minded and plan to compromise and occasionally do things that the other person wants.

As stated earlier, compromise is a two-way street, so if his idea of bonding is always doing the things he wants, you need to talk before you make commitments.

<u>Different Thought Process</u>: *Before you commit, ask the tough questions. If he gets uncomfortable, so what? You want to see him in as many different situations as possible so you know who you are dealing with. If you want a commitment and he doesn't, step away from the emotions of the moment and analyze yourself and the situation. Be honest, are you moving too fast? Are there loose ends that need to be addressed? Is your biological clock ticking too loud? If you can honestly answer these questions with no emotional input and you know you are not being premature in your request, you should consider moving on. Don't be engaged for fifteen years…*

VIII)Don't Lose Yourself

As you go through this journey we call life, you will come across different obstacles. Some will be bumps in the road while others can be devastating. Some you will be able to control while others you will have absolutely no control of.

The hardest obstacles to deal with are those you have no control over that turn out to be devastating, such as losing a loved one. While you cannot control this, you have to deal with it nonetheless.

Some people make life much harder than it has to be by making what should be a bump in the road escalate into pure devastation. Going up for a well-deserved job promotion and not getting it is a real downer but still only a bump in the road. It is not the end of the road and should have you moving forward with determination whatever your decision at that point turns out to be.

This is also true if a relationship ends. It can take you down to serious lows and have you doubting the very core of who you are. A breakup, though emotionally tough, if put in its proper perspective, is still only a bump in the road. This, however, is not the case for quite a few women. These women are devastated at the end of what might have been a good relationship. Why is this?

We have heard that in order to have a strong, long lasting relationship, one must fully commit and give oneself to the relationship. This can be true as long as you don't give control of who you are to the other person or to the relationship. You cannot afford to lose who you are in the blending process of a relationship. As previously discussed, no relationship is worth losing the essence of who you are.

It might feel good and comforting to give full control of the relationship (and thus yourself) to the man of your dreams who you think you can trust while you put it in neutral and bask in emotional bliss. By doing this you are hoping he will always do the right thing no matter what situations or pressures arise.

This is quite a gamble considering that any man, no matter how good, is still only human and thus always susceptible to the weaknesses of the human species—just like the rest of us. Commit to your relationship, but do not commit to turn over control of your life to anyone. Maintain control of your own life so if things don't go as planned even after years of commitment, the shockwave you experience will be more like a tremor than an earthquake.

Different Thought Process: *Maintain control of your life as this will allow you to create the balance that all strong relationships need. If a man insists on dictating everything in the relationship, thus killing the essence of who you are...keep him moving.*

The Chameleon is depending on your emotions to make your decisions as it then becomes easier for him to use his skill of emotional manipulation. If your emotional decisions benefit him, he will assure you that you are indeed doing the right thing. Be strong, maintain your self-worth, and practice emotional control.

IX)Set High Standards and Maintain Them

Most women understand the concept of having standards in their lives. Standards are the guide you use to hold others, including yourself, accountable. By doing this, you maintain a certain level of decorum in your life. Without these standards, your life becomes a "free for all," and you end up losing respect from others.

Without standards in place you have very little to guide you and you will go as the wind blows.

If a man sees you in the mall and gives you a compliment about your butt, what is your response? It is, after all, a compliment. Your response to his behavior will set the standard by which you allow this man and others to approach you. If your response is a smile or better, he now knows you are receptive to crass behavior and will log this for future reference should you allow him to get to know you.

By setting high standards, you will also be doing yourself a huge favor. Most Chameleons look for soft targets, so they want nothing to do with a woman who is firm about maintaining her standards. It goes to reason that if you maintain high standards, you will eliminate some Chameleons without even knowing it.

Most women do have standards; however, they tend to lower their standards depending on the situation. Usually, the "cuter" the guy, the lower the standard. How many times have you heard "damn, he's cute" in reference to a guy being hauled off in handcuffs? In the mall example above, some women's reaction will be based on how the guy looks. An open comment about her butt might make her spin around with venom, but if the guy is cute, she ends up smiling.

<u>Different Thought Process:</u> *You must be consistent with your standards. They cannot be high for some but lower for others. The act of lowering your standards is a guarantee you will be inviting a chameleon into your life. A man will show more respect to a woman who expects to be respected than one who just flows with whatever comes her way. Don't lower your standards; try elevating your expectations instead. Expect to be treated with dignity and with respect. Expect a man to show respect from the start and expect him to maintain this respect, otherwise...keep him moving.*

X)Don't Rush Into Relationships

Though it is a natural part of our culture to find a mate and move forward together, there should be no time frame in which to do so. In today's society, people are so quick to start serious relationships. If the vibe feels right after a few months and the friends approve, it's a done deal. It's better to take time to really get to know the other person and allow him to get to know the real you.

It's easy to deal with you when you are in a good mood and feeling great, but what about when you are a little under the weather or just in a downright lousy mood? Can he stand you then? Will he have the patience and compassion needed to weather this storm?

What about your bad habits? Will he be able to handle those? Will a pair of underwear hanging on the shower head send him flying off the handle? Or will it get him upset enough that it becomes the start of a bad day? You get the point? There are quite a few things you both need to find out about each other before you make hasty decisions.

Do you just give the keys to your car to any guy standing by the door of the restaurant or hotel and just hope he's the valet who works there? Probably not, even though it doesn't take long to establish that he is the valet after you give him the once over and make sure he's in uniform and doesn't look out of place, etc. Why then don't you do the same before you give the keys to your heart to the next pretty face that makes your knees wobbly? You owe it to yourself to step back from the situation and make sure this person has been properly vetted using your rational mind.

I guarantee that if you do give your keys to someone who eventually steals your car you will have the feeling (even for a fleeting moment) that something is wrong. We all get that feeling when we are about to take a gamble. Before you make any decision that can adversely affect your life, give yourself a STOP moment. Put the emotions on hold for a while then see if this is what you really want for yourself in the long term. If you cannot reach a definitive answer, this just means you need to take more time to get to know the other person. Continue to enjoy what the relationship offers and let time help to unravel some of the mysteries or issues that might be causing doubt.

Is this not a great situation to be in where you are enjoying the moments in your relationship and just letting them come to you?

A man can tell you what drives him and what his goals are, but you need to observe his lifestyle to verify if what he says is what he does. He will tell you what type of person he is, but situations will prove what he says to be either true or false. The problem is that some situations take time to arise. You should therefore allow time to be your friend. You also need to allow for enough time so you can both become friends.

What is the rush to start a serious relationship with someone who meets your expectations? Is this person such a catch that you don't want to run the risk of losing him? How much of a catch is he if he doesn't think *you* are a great catch yourself?

If he does think you are a catch, he will let you know by his actions that he won't be going anywhere anytime soon. This should allow you to relax and enjoy the moment and also give you time to see if he is genuine or just full of it.

If there is pressure to start a serious relationship, don't succumb to it. Instead, spend some time analyzing what is causing this pressure and why. It will be time well spent.

The Chameleon knows that the *perception* of a relationship fills some women's need to feel wanted. If the woman bites on this perceived relationship, The Chameleon will

Dameon Smith

have full access to her inner soul. Because she needs to feel wanted, she will quickly expose her inner being once she thinks she has found her dream man. Exposing one's inner soul is a signal to the other person that you are ready to take that next step in the relationship. Ideally, this must be done by both at the same time.

There is a sense of vulnerability that arises for both men and women when it's time to take the relationship to the next level, whether it's having sex, moving in together, introducing the partner to Mom and Dad, or an engagement. The realization hits home that what you are about to do is a big step, and a cause for pause is fully justified. Ideally, you want to start your relationship without any trepidation.

Women know that expressing their feelings early leaves them exposed and vulnerable, but many do it anyway. These women are slaves to their emotions. They allow their emotions to tell them "this feels good, let's try to lock it in." They then embark on an emotional suicide mission with their emotions leading the way.

During various interviews, I found that the women who are quick to express their feelings usually say, "I want a guy to know I'm not into playing games, so I just tell him how I feel." By doing this, she is gambling that the guy is not a Chameleon and will echo her sentiments and thus keep her happy emotions flowing. The problem with this thinking is that the woman exposing her inner feelings too early in a relationship has an air of desperation about her that makes most men shiver at the thought of being in a relationship with her. Her behavior will put a damper on whatever genuine feelings the man might have for her.

The Chameleon, however, being a skilled player who knows an easy target when he sees one, will tell her whatever she wants to hear. He will then take her and her emotions for the ride of her life and have her picking up the pieces in short order. This is not a gamble worth taking. Keep your emotions in check and let things flow naturally.

The tendency is to get carried away and start projecting how a long-term relationship with a new guy might be after going on just a few dates. If you start doing this, you will of course only be thinking of the good things, thus creating the perfect relationship in your head. Doing this will shut down your rational mind and all the defense mechanisms that you would normally use to filter out the players, the stalkers, and the nut-jobs.

You will be better served if you just let life come to you by allowing the situation to develop on its own while you enjoy the moment. In doing this, you are better able to manage your emotions and fully observe the actions of the other person.

Again, if this is the right man for you, he fully expects to have to prove that he is the right person for you. Allow him the opportunity to do what he knows is expected of him. If he is that man, everything will flow naturally. You will go through tough spots and recognize that they are tough spots, but somehow they will work themselves out without being major stresses in your life. Rein in your emotions and let him show himself worthy of being your partner. This can be difficult, because at this point your emotions are in full gear and you want to show how much care and how much affection you have for him.

But you must continue being the self-assured woman that you are so that it will all come together.

This process of developing a long-term relationship does not take a quick couple of months. It takes time because so many things will happen along the way that should give both of you pause. Once they are individually figured out, the journey continues.

<u>Different Thought Process</u>: *Enjoy the journey and do not concern yourself with getting too serious too early. Once he presents his case for a serious relationship, try to make as rational a decision as you can by eliminating emotions and then following your heart. The answer might very well be that you are just not ready for that kind of commitment at the moment. Don't be afraid to say so. It's in your best interest to wait until you are indeed ready.*

XI)Every Pot has a Cover

Have you ever noticed that even someone you consider mean-spirited, ugly, or selfish has a relationship that seems to work for her? How does this happen? Why is your average-looking friend with the bland personality in a seemingly happy relationship and you are not?

The first thing you should do when confronted by this is to not put any thought into someone else's situation. This will only serve to increase your frustration, causing you to make irrational decisions. You don't want to make a decision to be in a relationship just because all your friends are in one. Don't be jealous of your friends' relationships. Only they and God know what transpires behind closed doors. The picture they paint of their relationships is their business. This should only concern you if you plan on being a third party in their relationships. Focus on you! Never apologize for who you are and how you are living your life.

Your last relationship might not have worked out, but you must keep reminding yourself that "every pot has a cover," meaning: there is someone for everyone. Someone is out there who will increase your happiness and whose happiness you will increase, someone who will wipe your nose when you cry and tell you things to make you laugh through the tears. Someone who cares enough about you to make sacrifices for you and for whom you will do the same.

Know that your last relationship wasn't the last candy on the shelf. You need to remember that happiness lies within you and not in others. Wanting to share your happiness with someone else is natural but must not be forced. The person you choose to share your happiness with must also be happy with who he is and where he is in life. If he is not happy, he will suck the happiness from within you. His miserable behavior will make your formerly happy demeanor as miserable as his.

Whatever you do, do not get yourself locked into a position if you have any lingering doubts about the situation. A lot of times the urge might be to take the chance and fix this issue later. This is just your emotions wanting to keep the good feeling going, so shut it down and put your rational mind to work. It's one thing to not know of something but totally different to know and then ignore it. If you value your time, fix any issues you are aware of before you commit to a situation you might later regret.

Obviously if you know what you want, you will be able to recognize it when you see it. What someone else might perceive as a dominant person (large pot cover for them) might be just to your liking. Likewise, someone thought of as not manly enough for someone else (small pot cover for them) might just be your perfect fit. Recognizing the right fit for you is your decision. Others will observe your selection and give their opinions, but ultimately you will be the one living with the final decision.

No matter how your selection is perceived by others, as long as the person you have chosen validates your choice by proving to be who you thought he was, you will be able to live with your decision. Your aura will attract people who will love you just the way you are; it is then your responsibility to know who the right fit for you is and eliminate those who are not. This is a much better situation than waiting for someone else to "pick" you.

If you have ever watched kids pick teams for a pickup game you will understand the following dynamic. The two kids thought of as being the best at that particular event choose who they want to have on their respective teams. The quicker the other kids are selected, the more important they feel. It gives each kid a sense of being more highly thought of than the kids picked after them. The emotional fulfillment of being picked on the same team as certain other kids feels good. Some women seem to have carried this dynamic with them into their adulthood. They feel oh so special if chosen by a certain guy to be his date or his girlfriend, disregarding what little self-worth they might have had.

<u>Different Thought Process:</u> *You must lose this mindset and know that you should be the one doing the choosing. Let a man present his case to be with you; then and only then do you start the thought process to decide if he is worthy. Who knows better if this person is the right fit for you than you? In the meantime, keep enjoying your life without waiting for someone to select you.*

This choice of deciding after the man is a right that women have but many choose not to exercise. If they meet a man they like, they make it known and then hope the man chooses to move forward with them.

There is obviously no perfect man (or woman), but there is someone just right for you.

Chapter 4
Understanding Men

❧

Once you have "found yourself" by knowing who you are and what you want out of life, you will be better equipped to handle any issues that might arise during your life's journey. Finding yourself and meeting someone who has also found himself is a high percentage of brokering a successful relationship. When both of you know who you are as a person, chances are good it's going to be a smooth transition into a good, long-lasting relationship.

The other factors in making all this work is the tricky part. We have all seen two perfectly well-rounded people try to make a relationship work but fail miserably. Each will give varying reasons why the relationship failed but in the end will still not be too sure what the real reason was. These other factors encompass a variety of things, such as personality types, compatibility, chemistry, timing, understanding the opposite sex, etc.

Women who know themselves know what personality type they like in a man, whether he is laid back, energetic, social, or whatever. Given enough time, they can also figure out if they are compatible with someone. Knowing if you have chemistry with someone should be a no-brainer. There are other issues at play within these factors, but understanding how the opposite sex thinks seems to be the great divide and the one we will now address.

Understanding how those around you think and operate is so second nature to you that you don't usually give it a second thought. Since you have spent countless hours together, you know the thought processes of those close to you. You know which friend is most likely to give a sarcastic retort, who is more likely to pull a particular prank, or who will take home the stray puppy. When it comes to understanding the thought processes of men in regard to relationships, most women have never given this a second thought. Many just assume that as long as they are direct and honest, they should get a direct and honest response.

In order to understand men a little better you need to step outside yourself and view the situation from a man's perspective.

Most men do try to give a direct and honest response; however, many times the intended response gets lost in transition. Men are not known for expressing their feelings freely and many rely more on their actions to communicate e.g. gift giving. Some women will view this lack of verbal communication as the man shutting down, and in turn they start shutting down themselves. This can start a cycle that leads to major problems. If, however, you understand that men do communicate this way, then instead of shutting down, you can address the communication issues and move toward your desired resolution.

Be aware that men and women do see certain situations differently. Understanding how men see various things will give you a better understanding of why most respond a certain way to certain situations. Understanding how men think about sex, relationships, and commitment will help shine some light on the existing confusion some women experience. The Chameleon thrives on this confusion because it allows him the means to twist, turn, and rationalize his way into and out of most situations. Understanding men will also allow you to quickly analyze what is meant as opposed to what is said.

During the interview process, one of the most frequently asked questions by women was "Why do men like bitches?" Another area of query was "Why are men afraid of commitment?" Also, "What do men look for in a long-term relationship?'

I)Why Do Men Like Bitches?

When this question is asked, the impression is that men are jerks who will take a good woman for granted but chase after a rude, uncouth female.

Before you hurt your neck nodding affirmatively, let's take a closer look.

When a woman classifies the next woman as a "bitch" on the job, she is talking about that mean-spirited, self-absorbed individual who has crossed the line from self-confident into the realm of the obnoxious. This is not the "bitch" being referred to here. The "bitch" being referred to here is the woman classified as such because she doesn't cave in to others and possesses something that the other woman doesn't.

This "something" has nothing to do with material vanity, such as an expensive car or jewelry, nor does it have anything to do with social status. This "something" is basic, old self-confidence.

Dameon Smith

Having self-confidence causes this woman to have a certain aura about her. It is this aura that so intimidates the insecure woman that it causes her to label the other woman a bitch. This act of negative labeling is an attempt to hide the insecurity this other woman brings out in her. Negative labeling feels like the natural response in such a situation because it is our society's way of dealing with things we don't like or don't understand. Because of this mindset, many a good woman gets classified as a bitch.

So if you ask again "Why do men like bitches?" the answer should now be a little clearer. If not, let's bring the whole picture into focus.

A man and a woman will look at the same female but see two different people. Where the intimidated woman sees a bitch, the man will see this same woman for who she really is, i.e., someone who is confident and secure in who she is. At this point her social status means nothing. Whether a waitress at the local diner or a judge at the local courthouse, all a man will see at this point is someone who won't suck the life out of him. For most men this is a big deal since very few men want an insecure, needy woman. This is the reason so many men find confident women extremely sexy.

In contrast to a self-assured, confident woman, an insecure, needy woman will be quick to express how much she cares, how much love she has to give, or how great she is in a relationship. She will be quick to cough up the funds to support this man, whether it's to put him through school, nurse him through rough times, or simply pay his bills. To a man, this behavior comes off as desperate and weak since she is willing to spill her guts, make early commitments,

64

or open up about herself before really getting to know him. This is a big turn-off for most men as it leaves little to intrigue them about this type of woman. The only thing on his mind at this point is to follow the bread crumbs and back out of the relationship or conversation before he becomes trapped.

On the other hand, a woman with an air of confidence (a "bitch") poses a special predicament for a man. He first wants to find out what makes her think she is special then he wants to have her do the things she says or gives the impression she won't readily do.

During an interview, a young man told me he had a standard protocol of having the women he met visit his home and gauge their worth based on their reaction to the situation he had just put them in. Joe is what I call "organized chaos." His place, while clean, is unorganized, but he knows where everything is located. According to Joe, every woman who came to his place for the first time always had a comment or a "look" that needed clarification regarding his "mess."

If she volunteered to cleanup, he filed her under "nice" and allowed her to organize his mess but emotionally disconnected from her right away. If she volunteered to cleanup but requested his help, he filed her under "good" but declined the clean-up request because it was never about that. If she refused to acknowledge his mess, Joe spent all night trying to convince her to help him cleanup. According to him, he wanted the pleasure of making her do something she never thought she would do. As twisted as his system seems, that was his thought process, and it is the thought process (with some variations) of quite a few men.

A woman might meet a guy she likes and because of her insecurities thinks giving in to sex early will show him how much she likes him. To a guy, this kind of woman is considered *weak* if she gives it up too early.

During interviews, some men have told me that the time frame in which first-time sex occurs is irrelevant if you connect with the woman. Even if you think the connection is there, you don't know for sure until you get to know the other person better. Why gamble away your reputation instead of getting to know the other person? An added benefit of getting to know the guy better is that the time required for this will frustrate a "window shopper," causing him to eliminate himself.

Many more men confessed to initially having doubts about the level of challenge the woman posed if the sex came too soon.

As an example, if a woman caves in to sex within the first couple weeks, most of the men said they would consider her weak. They would accept the sex but don't plan on anything developing beyond that. If a guy thinks he has your ticket punched, in his mind you are done. If the woman holds out beyond a few weeks, as long as the guy doesn't think it's a waiting game and it's just a matter of time before she caves in, the potential is there for something to develop.

If while "holding out" the woman shows signs of being in control of herself (being a "bitch") and thus in control of the situation, more often than not this guy will be around trying to get more than sex *i.e. trying to find out what makes her tick.* In the time spent doing this, he will also be getting to know her. He will also be trying to win the mind game that *he* thinks is being played. His goal is now to try and break her mentally—this is a man's ego at work.

Most men are all about ego. For men, the little voice in their head is not usually their conscience but rather their ego, hence their competitive nature—who's got the fastest, prettiest, or biggest.

In order for a man to accomplish the goal of breaking a strong woman (a "bitch"), he must get into her head to figure out and change her thought process. The problem for him is that this is easier said than done. Because of her self-confidence, she will possess the necessary mental strength to allow access only where she wants when she wants. This causes a mental struggle with any guy trying to get into her head and a battle of wills to ensue. This does three things that work in the "bitch's" favor.

1 –He will think that "nothing good ever comes easy," so by her not being easy, it stands to reason that she must be a good catch. This elevates her value in his mind.

2 – By not being easy for him, he assumes she won't be easy for other guys, and this helps to soothe his insecurity about other men trying to get her. He will quickly try to put her on a pedestal out of the reach of other men.

3 – The perceived mental challenge that a "bitch" creates is in line with what drives men. Nothing gets a man going more than a challenge.

Challenges allow men to fulfill their competitive needs and soothe their egos. All men possess this competitive urge that, once realized, must be fulfilled. This becomes apparent when accolades are up for grabs. Whether a computer nerd who lives for hacking, a weekend warrior way past his prime but who still goes to the local park to compete, a boardroom bully who must have the last word, or participating in a simple barbeque cook-off—men are just competitive. It should be no surprise then that once a guy likes you, the easiest way to get and keep his attention is to address what his passions are while still being a challenge.

This is not to say you should go out there and *try* to be a challenge for anyone, because no one is worth that. *A "bitch" does this without trying!*

You should instead develop your self-confidence then let it shine through, and your reward shall be great. You should never *try* to be a challenge.

This is how it works: You must square away your self-confidence issues before you can move forward. Once you have done this, your self-confidence will have you believing that you are "it"—the female ego.

This confident feeling will improve your response to any situation. It will create an aura about you that will let others see that you are different. By being different, you create the perception of being a challenge. It is this perception that will make a man brand you as a challenge in his mind (that's on him). Since we all know that the mind is very powerful, allow his mind to do the work for you—all you need is to let your self-confidence shine through and let his mind do the rest.

Funny how it works; if you develop a love of self, others will be attracted to you.

Some women show this attitude at the beginning, but once they are in the relationship, they lose themselves trying to make the relationship work. A self-confident woman does not worry about such things; she simply lets it flow, and it is this relaxed "whateva" attitude that keeps the man intrigued. This is why it is imperative that you maintain who you are throughout any relationship. This way whatever you have that got him hooked in the first place will always be there. Furthermore, if you don't change, you can't be accused of changing, and whatever the outcome of the relationship, you will still love who you are because you never changed.

The value of a self-confident woman (a "bitch") remains high to a man because he recognizes and respects her self-esteem and independence.

II)Commitments – The Scary Truth

Women are often heard saying that men are scared of commitments. During the interviews, the guys I spoke with believed they sometimes have good reason for not wanting to commit. They don't view it as being scared but more so as being cautious.

Though there are men who use being "scared of commitments" as an excuse to drag women through years of agony or freeloading while they wait for their Miss Right, understand that these are just your Chameleons at work. There is, however, some validity to others who hesitate when the "c" word is uttered.

To commit or not to commit, that *is* the question men ask themselves before they decide whether or not to take the plunge. And a plunge it is indeed since no one truly knows where any relationship will lead.

The thought process of men is quite different on this subject than it is for women. When a newly engaged woman breaks the news of pending marriage to her girl-friends, more often than not the celebration and the touch-down dance begins and the only thing left to do is to spike the ball. On the other hand, when her fiancé gives his boys the news, you can hear a pin drop right before someone says, "Dude, are you sure you want to do this?"

Many dads and uncles have given young men the speech of living a little before they get married—don't tie yourself down too early, etc. Most young women, on the other hand, are expected to find a husband and start a family before they are too "old"—quite the contrast, don't you think?

The fact that girls mature faster than boys throughout adolescence and puberty is no secret. What is not often discussed is that a woman's biological clock is also more advanced than a guy's of the same age. This creates an unbalanced situation where you get one person who's confident and ready to settle down and another who's not so sure. The woman's confident feeling (buoyed by her biological clock) of being ready to settle down can make it seem as if she has an ulterior motive and scares the daylights out of a guy whose biological clock is not in sync with hers. Considering this, is there any doubt why a guy would be skeptical about getting married? No one wants to fail at anything, but men have stated that failing *miserably* is the real reason for their skepticism.

History has shown that many who have thought their relationships would stand the test of time have failed to do so. The idea of failing in a relationship (as stated above) is not what scares men. The idea of failing *miserably* is the nightmare most men dread. Failing at most things in life generally only requires you to dust yourself off and try again with your newly learned lesson to guide you.

Failing *miserably* in a relationship is when the breakup becomes explosive and bitterness and anger are added to the normal hurt that is usually involved. Once things get to this level, they usually cause splits between friends, the taking of sides, families getting involved, etc. As you may know, this is one ugly mess that can last for years. This is not even counting the years of financial ruin if marriage is involved.

All of the above repercussions of failing *miserably* are what scare the living daylights out of most men and why so many break out in cold sweat at the thought of committing. It is easy to jump in if you only focus on the positive, but as in other aspects of life, the whole picture must be taken into consideration, including the ramifications if things go awry.

A man will gladly enter into a relationship without hesitation if due diligence was done in analyzing the pros and cons. It is one thing to not know of an issue but a different story to know of it and just hope it works itself out. If either party knows of existing issues that might cause problems later, it makes sense to address them before moving forward. The stakes are too high to do otherwise. This is what any self-loving woman should want, as the man might uncover something that she missed that could save both of them from going down a road destined for colossal failure.

As an example, *let's say you think the relationship should be a committed one but he is shying away from that. Let's also assume you have both agreed you want nothing to do with kids. His not wanting to commit could be him having second thoughts about wanting kids and not sure he'll be able to convince you otherwise. Wouldn't it be beneficial to you for him to hesitate about committing so you can both discuss the situation rather than jumping into a commitment because it would make you happy? Doing otherwise might feel good now, but later it may cause problems because you are not on the same page.*

Some women know about current issues but are of the mindset that "love conquers all." They will keep going forward full steam ahead hoping that love does save the day. This flawed ideal is advocated by Chameleons far and wide as they recognize that once a woman leaves it to love to cure all ills they now have a license to act the fool in this woman's life. "Why would I do that? You know I *love* you!" Sounds familiar?

How then does a woman know if her man has a legitimate concern or whether he is just a Chameleon using "I'm scared of commitments" to string her along? If at the mention of making it a committed relationship the man goes on the defensive, don't panic. Maybe he knows you guys are not ready to take that step at the current time. You, however, must let it be known that "we need to talk about this." If he agrees to discuss the situation, then you can both discuss the issues at hand and see where doing so leads. If he refuses to talk about it and blows it off as you rushing him, pressuring him, or the like, he either needs to work on his communication skills (which should be of concern to you) or you have yourself a Chameleon who is just buying time waiting for a better situation to pop up.

III) Relationships – A View from the Other Side

Women who "know" will tell you that guys are easy to read. You just need to keep *your* emotions in check for a while so you can see what gets *his* emotional juices flowing. Too often women get so caught up with their own emotions that they fail to observe what emotions the man is showing in certain situations (men have feelings too). Sometimes a woman needs to pull back a little from the moment so she can observe the man in his emotional state. Once she knows what gets him going, she is in a better position to control the situation or at least to not be overwhelmed by it.

When it comes to what men want in a long-term relationship, there are quite a few wants, but most fall under three basic and simple headings:

1. <u>A woman who has inner strength</u>: A man wants a woman he can lean on when he is at his lowest and is willing to go through thick and thin with him. A woman who will provide needed support when he is not at his best. One who will see him at his weakest moment and instead of using it to emasculate him, will take over and help boost him back to his normal state.

Her inner strength will also allow him to exhale because he doesn't feel he has to be Superman every day. It also shows that she is comfortable in her own skin and doesn't need him to validate her—this gives a man peace of mind. This mental peace allows a man to be in his comfort zone because it provides breathing room.

Men need breathing room to avoid the feeling of being governed by a leash law. Even though a man might be out of his partying stage, he still wants to know he can go hang with the boys from time to time without being henpecked about it.

Having breathing room provides balance for both men and women, and this is good for any relationship. Allowing a man room to breathe also gives the woman time to catch *her* breath so she doesn't get consumed by the relationship.

Think about a time when you had someone around you who wanted you to spend all your free time with him. That suffocating feeling is why both men and women need time apart even if it's just in a different part of the house. Oddly enough, if a man doesn't feel pressured when he goes out, he doesn't have any trepidations when it's time go home.

2. <u>A woman who can be his best friend</u>: In order to be a best friend there must be trust, mutual respect, and understanding regardless of the parties involved. Being a best friend means she won't judge him in spite of his quirks or pet peeves but will instead do things that shows she understands—this allows him to be himself. Being a best friend means being able to act the fool without feeling like a fool.

Because of the trust involved, a best friend is usually open-minded and receptive to new ideas without being judgmental. This will help to keep the relationship fresh, fun, and interesting. Being a best friend, the man knows she will understand him. This means he won't have to spell out everything to her; she just knows or will trust his judgment if she doesn't. A man wants the trust and respect to be such that if he's out with his friends, she is not calling and saying "tell me you love me" just to gauge if there are women in the group. If there are indeed women in the group, he wants a woman who trusts him enough to know there is nothing to worry about.

I'm sure you have seen older couples that are so close it makes you smile every time you see them. You understand this kinship because it reminds you of good times with best friends.

Now the complicated part:

3. <u>A woman who understands what sex means to him</u>: Many people tend to assume that sex is sex and that the next person wants it the same as they do. Because of this mindset, sexual compatibility usually is assumed and thus gets shoved to the back burner. A man wants a woman who is sexually compatible so that the sex will keep flowing. From a man's perspective, this should be an easy enough task that requires little effort. So why then is this such a big deal in so many long-term relationships? Men have stated that even after sexual compatibility has been determined, the sex dries up after the woman gets comfortable in the relationship. The joke that "the worst food for a woman's sex drive is her wedding cake" rings true to quite a few men.

   Some of the men I interviewed have even wondered if the women faked sexual compatibility to seal the deal then left them high and dry once the relationship was perceived as being secure.

   For their part, the women have responded that their men stopped doing the little things that made them feel special and sexy so their interest in sex is not what it used to be. In response, men have stated that a woman wearing a head full of curlers and her granny's underwear does nothing for them.

Regardless of whose action came first, it is obvious that there is a divide between how men and women view this subject.

Generally speaking, and the occasional quickie notwithstanding, a woman usually cares how you lead up to sex: timing, mood, etc., whereas all a man usually needs is a time and a place...and it's on. Sex for most men does not involve as much detail as it does for most women. This fundamental difference in approach can create problems and is enough for most women to get tired of the same old stuff.

All that being said, all a man wants is sex when he wants it. Some men have stated that they don't mind doing the romantic "thing," but that it gets old fast because few women ever want to surprise *them* with romance.

Men also want women who won't withhold sex as a weapon of retaliation. For men, this is playing dirty and is cruel and unusual punishment since they believe women can voluntarily be sexual camels (no sex for long stretches). In a man's mind, women can go without sex for long stretches with no problem whereas for men it takes quite a bit of effort to survive this cruel fate of restricted sex.

Men do understand that there might be physiological reasons why a woman might not feel like having sex but still can't understand why she doesn't do it anyway; how hard can it be!?! It can be that puzzling.

Men want a woman who will make time for sex instead of using the kids or work, etc. as an excuse to say she is not in the mood. If that's not possible, one who will at least give him future hope instead of just shutting him down.

To sum up a man's view for keeping the sex flowing: Help to keep the passion going so the flames keep glowing—surprise him with romance every now and then. Be open-minded to new things and enhance the old things, such as mental foreplay, to keep him engaged. And finally, don't let yourself go—take care of both your mind and body.

Do understand that all of the above are what a man will say he wants. What he actually needs might be quite different, but to him his wants *are* his needs and should not be taken for granted. What you give him will depend on the situation and the returns. You must both be on the same wavelength: he must "get" you and you must "get" him. Obviously a proper solution can only be had through dialog between both parties.

IV)The Woman of His Dreams

A man isn't likely to settle if he doesn't think you are "The One," and you usually can't wear him down. If you do, you are setting yourself up for a miserable life where you must constantly sacrifice in order to keep him happy.

All men, *all men* want to put the woman of their dreams on a pedestal if given the opportunity. He wants her to know she's "The One" and he doesn't care what anyone else thinks. He will do whatever it takes to make her feel special. Of course the woman of *his* dreams might not give him that opportunity because she doesn't see him as the man of *her* dreams. Most women have felt this special feeling at some time or other. Many times for women this attention comes from the wrong person and they wish, *If only Michael felt this way about me.*

Invariably, if the guy she likes puts her on a pedestal, she will never forget him. Ask any woman what was so different about that guy and she will tell you, "He made me feel special."

If a man does not put you on a pedestal and makes you feel like you're "The One," you are NOT the one for him—*believe this.* Conversely, just because a man puts you on a pedestal doesn't mean you are "The One." The Chameleon is a great juggler worthy of being in any circus and can easily maintain two or three pedestals at the same time for the women of his dreams.

While you are on that pedestal, however, you will be able to enjoy all those perks and the feelings that come with being put there. Enjoy these as you move forward to investigate if there is any truth behind his words and actions. He could be "The One," but you cannot allow yourself to be caught up in the moment just because he is treating you as if you were special. If you get lost in the moment, you may end up picking yourself off the floor after the rug gets pulled from under you. No matter the feelings you are enjoying at the moment, always keep things in perspective by making sure your rational mind has not been shut down.

The Chameleon knows that making a woman feel special will stir her emotions, and he will do anything to start the emotional ball rolling. He will put you on the highest pedestal if he thinks this will make your emotions do your thinking for you.

The goal of all Chameleons is to get a woman to the point where her emotions are making her decisions. Once a woman is blinded by her emotions, The Chameleon can now lead her as he pleases.

A good analogy on the way men approach women would be the advice you get when going fishing. You are told not to fight the fish on the line but to enjoy the moment as you slowly reel it in. Sometimes you have to actually give it some slack before you start winding it in again. The greater the challenge in reeling in this catch, the more appreciation one has for the fight in the fish. God forbid this catch rises out of the water and appears to be "the big one." The catcher will then do his best not to lose this battle, and a prayer goes up with each twist and turn that occurs. Once it has been reeled in, if this fish is what the catcher had hoped for, he will be inclined to have it mounted as a trophy for all to see.

Being the trophy wife is an aspiration for many women. Unlike the fish tale above, a woman does have the option of choosing which "hook" she bites. Also, unlike the tale above, the "catcher" does get to see his "catch" before he starts to reel it in. The knowledgeable woman understands that to keep a man interested, a challenge must exist. While she won't be splashing around like a hooked fish, she understands that the line must have some resistance in order to keep both parties interested in the situation. She will allow the man to do what men like to do by allowing him to pursue her.

If you show your true self and the man sees you as "the big one," he will try to reel you in quickly for fear a "bigger fish" will snatch you off his line. His main goal from this point forward is to win you over, put you on a pedestal, and make you his trophy. For the most part, how you handle the situation determines the longevity of what transpires.

The key ingredient to a lasting relationship is both individuals continuing to make the other feel special.

V)Men Are Simple

Men are not complicated unless they want to deceive. If a man is really into a woman, he will generally break it down as simply as he needs to without necessarily telling her—his actions will let her know his intentions. He will absolutely leave some intrigue intact to keep it spicy but will not create doubts in her mind because he is just as scared of messing up as she is.

On the other hand, if you are not his Miss Right, he will be as evasive and devious as he thinks he needs to be in order to deceive you and get his way (The Chameleon). Many times a man's evasive or "don't care" behavior might seem intriguing and a source of attraction for some women. This kind of evasive behavior is nothing but smoke and mirrors to distract you from looking through the haze and seeing who he really is.

The Chameleon knows that people tend to chase things with more effort if those things are *just* out of their reach. Looking ahead and savoring the self-gratification that usually follows the successful end of any chase only intensifies the effort made during the chase. It is this same principle that is used to get greyhounds to run as hard as they can every time they step on the track. If the fake rabbit is placed too far ahead, they will chase it, but not as hard as if it's *just* out of reach.

A knowledgeable, self-assured woman knows this principle and uses it to her advantage. Instead of fawning over and chasing a man she likes, she instead keeps herself just out of his reach, thus controlling the tempo of the encounter. She is now the one perceived as intriguing.

Though a relationship is not a game, there is undoubtedly some mind play that naturally occurs as each individual processes, analyzes, and adjusts to the pros and cons of the current situation. You do not want to involve yourself with mind games, but analyzing the situation is a must. How else will you determine if the current situation is what you want it to be? Assuming you are not a mind reader, you have no idea what the other person's intentions are; therefore, at the beginning, there is only one person you can trust to treat you right and that's *you*.

Surely you don't intend to let the man tell you that this is the right situation for you. The problem is that some women do just that. They bask in the warmth of emotional bliss while allowing the man to take the relationship wherever he chooses. By the time they come to their senses the relationship is usually over punctuated by "it's not you, it's me."

At the core, men are fairly simple, but because of the different mindsets and communication issues between men and women things can get complicated.

During an interview session, for example, some women stated that it is easier for them to forgive physical cheating than it is to forgive emotional cheating. The problem during the ensuing debate was that for most of the men emotional cheating didn't even register. "What is that?" they asked.

After much back and forth, one lady asked, "How would you feel if I divulged the secrets of your poker game or what makes your modified car go fast to another man?" This got their attention because she had broken the barrier and was now talking in terms that let them better understand that a relationship with someone else doesn't have to be physical to drive a wedge between a couple.

According to these same women, the feeling of being betrayed and deceived is just as hurtful in an emotional relationship as it is in a physical relationship because of the intimate thoughts being shared. In addition, an emotional relationship creates a special bond and requires emotional energy that should only be shared with one's partner and thus usually leads to a physical relationship anyway.

The women went on to say that if the energy had been invested into their relationship in the first place there would not have been the need for the men to go elsewhere. The men's response was that some women tend to take a man's feelings and emotions for granted and it is this neglect that causes the void that leads to emotional release elsewhere. Obviously the importance of proper communication within a relationship comes to the forefront in situations like these.

Unless you are a practicing psychiatrist, the above scenario is best left to professionals. Can you "fix" him if you know that he wasn't hugged as a child or if he sat on "Uncle" John's lap once too often? Leave that kind of work to the pros. It might be tempting to figure him out and try to fix him, but resist the urge to do so. The self-gratification you might get from this experiment pales in comparison to the hurt and angst you will experience should it blow up in your face. How many women have you seen spend countless years sticking out a bad situation because they knew they could "help him"? Don't let "time served" convince you to keep moving forward with him. Figuring out who he is versus who he says he is will be time consuming enough.

Sometimes the chemistry between two good people is such that one just brings out the bad in the other. Often after parting ways, others are surprised to see how well each has moved on with someone else.

If it becomes a repetitive pattern of arguments for whatever reason and then being sorry about the argument, the simple relationship has now become an issue that requires professional intervention, or else you just need to move on. If it doesn't flow, let it go.

VI)Showing He Cares
Men tend not to communicate their feelings the way most women would like. Whether this is derived from

their upbringing or to maintain the appearance of a certain image, it is the way it is.

According to some of the men interviewed, they are more than willing to show that they care but get frustrated after too many failed attempts. Knowing that you are trying only to find out that you missed the mark—again—is what they say kills their spirits and causes them to shut down. Communication is the key here.

If you like to be surprised, make sure your partner knows your likes and dislikes. Otherwise a well-meaning surprise will end up disappointing you both. If, for example, you are a shoe fanatic who wears heels but not flats, a surprise pair of good-looking expensive flats won't have you doing cartwheels. Your subdued reaction will cause him to feel like a failure; thus you both will be a little deflated.

You might think you can fake a surprised happy reaction, but as good as you might be at faking in the bedroom, those skills won't help in this situation. For one thing, this time he's in his rational mind anticipating your reaction, so he will be better able to spot any fake enthusiasm. Secondly, this time he does care if your enthusiasm is for real.

If a man spends the time to surprise you, he wants to see an ecstatic reaction. To avoid the uncomfortable situation of trying to fake such a reaction and getting exposed, men have suggested that meaningful hints go a long way in solving this little dilemma. That vague hint you mentioned in passing three months ago means nothing if it is not later connected to something more concrete. Commenting about needing time away from the job, for example, does not translate into a trip to Jamaica unless you give meaningful hints (or just say so). What it does mean is that you want to get away to clear your head, so if you get tickets on a Greyhound to go see the countryside don't get angry. Help your partner out by properly steering him in the direction of what works for you. Playing CSI by trying to piece clues together can and does get old, so don't make it so hard to please you.

A genuine man does care, but as with anything else, there is a point of diminishing return. If he is trying but keeps coming up short again and again, he will eventually stop trying. Knowing each other and proper communication is a must!

Guys understand that the spoken word is the preferred medium of communication with women, but most agreed that sometimes they expect their partner to know that they care by the things they do, i.e., if he goes shopping with you, he cares. If he picks up your feminine products while at the supermarket, he cares. If he listens to and shares in your office politics and issues, he cares. If he tries to fix issues within the relationship, he cares. If he introduces you to his friends or family, he cares. If he defends you whether from strangers, friends, or family members, he cares. If he cancels his boys' night out for you, he cares. To a woman these might seem like trivial things, but a guy wouldn't even think of doing them, as simple as they may seem, if he didn't care.

Most of the men thought the above examples, among others, were *obvious* signs that they cared, or as one individual put it, "Do we have to jump off a cliff?" Think for a moment what your reaction would be if your significant other did any of the above for another woman. More than likely it would be something along the lines of "why are you doing *that* for *her?*" accompanied of course with the *a-t-t-i-t-u-d-e* that goes along with such questions.

Just because a man doesn't say "I love you" everyday doesn't mean he doesn't love you. To him, it's just like most things—it can lose value if overexposed. So to a guy the small things in between should show a woman that the love is still intact even though the words are not said. Does a kiss on the cheek in the morning have to be followed by "love you"? From a guy's standpoint the answer is no, the act speaks for itself. Some of the women interviewed said that although it's not a must, it would be nice to follow with the words every now and then.

Try to understand that most mature men dislike overbearing relationships and in turn try not to be overbearing in their actions. There is something to be said about appreciating the subtle things in life, such as a slight versus a direct touch, a light scent of fragrance versus an overpowering dousing of the same, or a partially revealing dress versus stripper wear.

At the beginning of a relationship, a woman wants proof that a man's intentions are indeed genuine. Saying things and then backing them up with actions provides the confirmation most women need. A man who is really interested is usually quite clear about his intentions and validates his words by his actions. He knows that a woman will better grasp his true intentions by him doing as opposed to just saying. Once this verification is complete, it's mostly about her emotions from that point forward.

Some men in long-term relationships might assume that taking care of "business" financially and physically should be enough proof that he cares. Ignoring the all-important emotional side of a woman is where most genuine men drop the ball. This is why a woman who appears to have everything will risk it all for a guy who caters to her emotional needs even when she knows she is just someone on the side for this guy.

How a man makes a woman feel by paying attention to her interests and passions, doing or saying certain things, sharing his feelings with her, listening to her, etc. are all important to her. Not being as emotionally grounded as women, many men over time default to only their actions to show they care instead of also continuing to implement the spoken word. While their intentions might be good, it can leave a void that leads to bigger issues in the relationship if not properly addressed.

The power of the spoken word is on display every day. Women fall for hollow promises and cling to faded dreams because of the words spoken to generate emotions and hope. Chameleons are masters of the spoken word and use this skill to evoke emotions.

Many relationships have ended prematurely because of not knowing how to communicate with the other partner. In his mind, a man might think he's doing what he should by taking care of "business" while the woman thinks he doesn't care anymore because he doesn't say the things he used to say or vice versa. Quite often, as stated above, men do things and expect the woman to know that this is his way of showing that he cares. This might work for couples that have been together for eons but can get lost in younger relationships because the dynamics are different.

Knowing how to communicate with your partner is very important. Initially this situation can be like trying to explain something to someone who speaks a different language. Both are trying to grasp what the other is saying and it can become frustrating because the connection cannot be made. With effort from both sides, this connection can be made and will end up creating a stronger bond once successful.

A man showing that he cares is a requirement before moving forward—if he is in love with you, he will show that he cares.

VII)Sex and the Modern Man

"All men think about is sex first, sex second, and all else is third."

The validity of this common perception among women was posed to some men during my interviews. For the most part a majority of the men stated that since sex does play an important role in any possible relationship, they like to get it out of the way (imagine that) then see if there is anything else beyond that. They reasoned that if the sex is not to their liking, why stay and endure the frustration of something you knew of beforehand? Once the sex part is covered, they can then move forward to see if there is enough to sustain a relationship. If not, they would rather leave than go through the motions just to say they are in a relationship. This, they say, is why it might seem as if men are just going around using women.

The idea of going around "sampling" might be an ideal scenario for men, but it is obviously not ideal for women. Oddly enough, a number of women admitted to falling for this "okeydoke" attitude of getting the sex out of the way. The men further stated that getting sex out of the way allows those involved to "put their cards on the table" because most women won't show their true selves until after sex because after that moment there is nothing else to hide.

If a relationship is broken down into sex and substance, of course a man will want to get the sex taken care of first. This is in his best interest. Even if the woman is deemed as not having what it takes and he must move on, getting sex upfront justifies time spent. Can you really blame a man for looking out for himself? Not really; however, you also need to be looking out for yourself by making sure you are not being taken for a ride.

Whatever clever ways guys come up with to justify early sex, it is up to you as a woman to flip the script to maintain some balance in such situations. Do not leave it up to the man to decide if you are worthy. He must know that you have standards and that you expect him to bring some substance to the table. This lets him know that he must invest time to obtain any type of decent return.

If he leaves at this point, good for you, you have just eliminated a chameleon. If he says he is willing to get to know you, it is now your responsibility to make sure he is not just playing the waiting game and is truly interested in getting to know you. Quality time spent together will assist in this endeavor.

Even though women are closing the gap at lightning speed, men are still a little better at separating feelings from sex. This is not necessarily a good thing, but it is what currently exists in our society. The ability to separate sex and feelings allows one to move from partner to partner in short order without much emotional baggage. What it also brings is a serial dater mentality as this person has found a way to justify not committing.

One justification for being noncommittal as stated during an interview is that men tend to be adrenaline junkies and that the adrenaline rush of not just sex but "new sex" (first time with a new partner) is what drives many men. There is no denying the adrenaline rush involved when you are with someone you connect with. Think about your first time with someone you really liked. The moments before the act (foreplay) are usually very intense. These intense moments are what these Chameleons (serial daters) say they try to recreate every time thereafter.

Another justification was explained as sex being the end result of a higher high where the act of sex itself is just validation that a mind game has been won. In this instance, it is not so much about the sex but more about the man's ability to get inside a woman's head. Sex is just confirmation that the mission has been accomplished. Women with confident personalities or those with social standings higher than the man tend to be the targets of this type of behavior. The Chameleon engaging in this type of behavior sees these women as conquests and gets his adrenaline rush from having these women do things they said or implied they would never do.

Because you don't want to end up with a serial dater, sex addict, or ego maniac, it is your responsibility to make sure the man's head is in the right place. Slow it down so you can better analyze the situation.

It is not as complicated as it might seem. For a man, new sex provides an emotional high. What differentiates the man who sticks around from the one who moves on is what the woman has to offer beyond sex. Though women stated that some men stick around just for the sex and this can be true, they never stick around forever just for the sex.

If all you have to offer is sex, a man will take it until he finds a woman who offers more before moving on, one who challenges him beyond the bedroom and gets his mind going on a level above his waist. At this stage sex becomes icing on the cake and is now used to show how much he enjoys the woman's company.

As stated before, never *try* to be a challenge. Your normal persona must naturally stimulate this man's mind and create the spark needed to get him fired up about wanting to know more about you.

As opposed to making sex the focal point of your relationship, try keeping the focus on getting to know each other. Sex only serves to get emotions fired up on both sides and can lead to misguided thoughts such as making "really like" seem like "love."

Chapter 5
The Mind is *Your* Business

❦

I) <u>The Mind Game</u>

Most of the women I spoke with admitted being tired of the mind games that some guys play. "Why can't they just be upfront and transparent?" they asked. Some of the men explained that the answer is twofold. First, what women see as "mind games" is their way of testing a woman's mettle. Second, the process itself creates an emotional rush that men like.

The reasoning goes like this: *The need to test a woman's mental strength, intentions, or level of commitment is brought about mostly by past experiences. If you have had a failed experience in the past, it is only natural to try to learn from your mistakes. The "mind games" are their way of eliminating those deemed not compatible with their goals, beliefs, or emotions. A few of the men stated that though some men do use mind games just for the emotional rush, that fact doesn't preclude them from using it to protect themselves from additional failed relationships.*

One guy mentioned that when he met his first girlfriend in high school, mind games were not necessary because neither of them had any past hurt to protect so they entered the relationship on pure emotions. He stated that once that relationship failed, he knew what to look for in personality types, etc. to prevent going down the same road in the future, and mind games allow him to accomplish this.

It is hard to disagree with someone who claims to be protecting himself. Whether it is the fear of being hurt, the uncertainty of the situation, or intentionally seeking a mental rush, mind games need to be differentiated from mental challenges. Mind games are an excuse to indulge in cheap thrills. If a man legitimately wants to know where you stand on any particular subject, there are civil, stimulating, and entertaining ways of doing so. These are mental challenges. Anyone who partakes in mind games usually has an ulterior motive and is actually exposing his personality type to others who are astute enough to pay attention. In fact, the first sign of mind games should set your chameleon alarm off.

While all men and women should analyze any situation in which they are in to verify the correct path, compatibility, etc., this can and must be accomplished without playing mind games. Don't waste time overanalyzing any situation that is cloaked in riddles or uncertainty; this is The Chameleon's playground. Instead, just keep living your life and let him worry about what you might be thinking. If his mysterious ways continue over time, it would behoove you to move on.

It can be a fine line, but mind games must not be confused with mental challenges. Within the context of a relationship, mental challenges are used to stimulate those involved, whereas mind games are used to confuse or gain an advantage over someone.

II) The Perfect Couple Rational Mind and Fate

Anything that happens can be attributed to fate. Does this mean we do nothing while we wait for fate to take us wherever? Of course not! Much like other things in life, fate coexists with our ups and downs and comings and goings. Saying "it must be fate" seems to be a convenient way to make decisions that benefit us. For example, if you are broke and find a purse with a couple hundred dollars, is this fate? Is it fate when you are in the produce department and you reach for a shiny red apple the same time the "handsome" guy next to you does? What if this guy is "ugly"? Is it fate then?

It is all fate, but what you choose to do with such random encounters is a choice, and this choice can then affect your life going forward *i.e. your destiny.* Opening a line of communication for one person and not the next is a choice you make that could significantly impact your life. If you choose to engage the guy in the produce department in conversation, this simple act can indeed change your destiny—hopefully for the good. We all know that a simple conversation can lead to dating, marriage, and kids, but you must first make the choice to converse for that to happen.

Some women like leaving these situations up to fate—"whatever happens, happens." This thought process usually occurs when they have a "feeling" the situation might not be the best for them but still want to satisfy their raging emotions. Blaming it on fate is an easy way to pass the buck should their suspicions prove to be true. It may be accurate to say fate put the woman in that situation, but by not making the rational decision to give time a chance to work, she has made the decision to gamble on her destiny by succumbing to her emotions. This is quite a gamble and one all chameleons hope their prospects will take.

In a perfect world, leading with your emotions would be the thing to do, but our world has people (e.g. salesmen or chameleons) who are hoping you do lead with your emotions so their job of convincing you becomes that much easier. Having emotions in your decision making is not always a bad thing, but you must temper these with rational thoughts. Regardless of the situation fate puts you in, it is better to make your decisions with some rational input rather than sheer emotions alone.

Sometimes you might get involved in situations that catch you by surprise—"didn't see that one coming." That is just life. Stuff happens, like the married guy skilled at hiding his situation until you have made certain commitments. If this occurs, your best choice at this point is to cut your losses and move on. Your emotions might be telling you to take him from his wife or to key his car, but unless you implement some rational thoughts into the situation, you will most likely be on the wrong path.

In other words, fate might have put you in whatever situation you are in, but the choices you make create your destiny. This is where rational thought plays an important role. Knowing that you are shaping your destiny with each decision, wouldn't it be better to have some rational thoughts involved to balance emotionally based decisions?

III) Mastering Your Emotions

All the different types of men with all their different styles of attracting a partner or just getting laid boils down to one thing…emotions. If you stir the emotions in a man, you have his attention. He in turn will want to get and keep your attention. He will try to do so by getting *your* emotions going, whether by stimulating conversation, being a "character," being different, or just making you laugh. The goal is the same—to get *your* emotions to join the party.

Creating emotional rush is the easiest way to keep anyone engaged in any situation (keep in mind that it doesn't have to be sexual).For example: *If you are in a business meeting that determines who gets kept and who gets laid off, it's guaranteed that emotions will be high and everyone will be paying attention.*

Even if you don't stir a man's emotions and he just wants to get laid (remember some men are good at separating sex and emotions),he will still be trying to get your emotions going because it makes his job easier.

Emotions are what endear us to each other. If you don't get that "feeling" when you meet someone for the first time, the chances are greatly reduced that they will get beyond the friendship level. That being said, emotions can slowly manifest themselves over time as well, causing someone to grow on you as you find out more and more about him.

Most people prefer getting that "feeling" right away as opposed to liking someone over time. This is understandable since the first scenario causes a blood-pumping, heart-racing emotional rush. This giddy feeling is what you want to experience again and again, causing you to anticipate your next interaction with the other person. Most men and women understand the addictive behavior of "wanting more" that is created by this emotional rush and know that it takes a lot of strength to resist making fools of themselves.

While most men and women try to enjoy the moments and afterglow created by this emotionally charged situation, The Chameleon's sole purpose is to use it to advance his agenda. He knows, for example, that introducing a measured amount of alcohol to the mix is the recipe for your basic one-night stand. He knows this encourages the woman to let go and have her emotions calling the shots.

If The Chameleon has long-term plans for this woman, he knows that his best chance of pulling off his con is to keep the emotions at a high level until she succumbs and starts making emotionally based decisions.

Once this level of emotion has been experienced, she will want to keep it flowing hard and fast because it feels so good. It's like an itch that needs to be scratched over and over. She will want to keep hitting this high again and again just like any other addiction.

Raw, unfiltered emotion is like a drug; it can take you to the highest high, and we all love the feeling. This is why men try to hit that emotional chord with women, because once reached, the need for continuation is great. When a woman meets someone who gets her to that high level of emotion, she is quick to throw caution to the wind and "let it rip" because this emotional drug is calling her name. The rational mind is then kicked to the curb as it would only serve to put a damper on her current euphoria. The only problem with doing this is that you don't yet know the full intention of the other person involved, and in heightened moments like these, the rational mind is all you have to protect you from yourself.

Just as emotions can take you to super-high levels, they can also take you to super-low levels. These low levels can be devastating on the psyche and lead to uncharacteristic behavior, depression, or even suicide. This is why no matter how much emotion you feel building within, you must be rational in your thought process so you can maintain control of said emotions.

It is easier to reap the emotional benefits from any new situation when things are going good and flowing fast than to slow it down and maintain control, so most people keep the fast flow going so they can enjoy the rush. When the pace is fast, the emotions are amped up since there are little to no checks and balances to slow it down. Slowing it down takes strength since this means reducing some of the emotions—no easy task. Slowing it down is, however, a good thing for you since you can't take anyone at face value when your emotional wellbeing is on the line, regardless of what *they* might say. Not every smiling face can be trusted. This is a dilemma that frustrates many women—how do you enjoy this feeling without being taken advantage of?

Your emotions will do anything to keep themselves going. They will make you think so much about the positives that you overlook the negatives even though the negatives outweigh the positives. This will cause you to create the perfect situation in your head when a closer look would have exposed the flaws. It is OK to go back and analyze a situation, but do so with a rational mind. However, don't keep thinking about it because then you might convince yourself of something that isn't really there.

Know that you can indeed enjoy any situation that stirs your emotions as long as you don't allow those same emotions to start making your decisions. This only shuts down your rational mind. It is a great feeling to let loose and let it all hang out, but this should be done once you have mastered your emotions.

Not making emotional decisions *is mastering your emotions.*

Not allowing your emotions to carry you off on some fairytale trip before the situation even has a chance to gain traction *is mastering your emotions.*

Remaining calm and not acting giddy even though your heart feels like it wants to jump out of your chest *is mastering your emotions.*

Basically you want to be like a duck in the water where your emotions might be working overtime like the duck's feet but on the surface all appears calm as you smoothly keep moving forward.

If you have not mastered your emotions, these same emotions will solicit the gambler in you in order to accomplish the task of keeping the emotions flowing. When something inside you is telling you to stop because something doesn't feel right, your inner gambler is saying "what the hell, go for it." Obviously the promise of splendor layered with emotions and topped with pure bliss is hard to resist, so you make the leap and hope for the best. This is a gamble that occasionally pays off, but more often than not it is followed by regret and self-loathing—"Why the hell did I do that?"

Eliminating Mr. Wrong

Emotional decisions bring more intense feelings than rational decisions because they are amplified by the anticipation of instant gratification. However, contrary to popular beliefs, euphoria and rational thinking are not mutually exclusive. The level of emotion you experience once you decide to move forward using your rational mind is only slightly less intense than taking a blind leap because the instant gratification is gone. Your emotions will, however, return to euphoric levels because your rational decision comes with a deeper sense of satisfaction and the added benefit of peace of mind, which allows you to fully enjoy your experience without second guessing yourself—this, as we all know, is a great feeling.

We have all had experiences that couldn't be fully enjoyed or that were cut short because of lingering doubt regarding the decision that was made—unprotected sex comes to mind. Getting married at city hall or in a Las Vegas chapel to someone you don't know enough about is another in a long list of snap decisions that brings along self-doubt.

Buying a car is another highly emotional decision that can bring regrets depending on the process used and closely parallels the relationship process. *If you go to a car dealership with the intention of going home with a car that day, the minute you see the one you want, your emotions start rolling as you anticipate driving it home. The car salesman is trained to cater to your emotions and will try to heighten them so that they assist **him** in your decision making. This salesman will market the same car in different ways depending on who the prospective buyer is, trying to hit that right emotional chord. This same car* *will be fast for a man, space efficient for a mom, safe for a senior, or sexy for a younger person.*

If after seeing the car you want you decide to leave so you can think about it, you have reduced the emotions a little and can better decide if this is actually the car for you. Upon your return to the dealership a day or two later, you will still have high emotions, but you will also have the added comfort of knowing that your decision now includes some logic. This will prevent you from cursing yourself or the car every time you head to your parking spot as opposed to looking back and smiling every time you walk away from the car. The pessimists among us will read this and ask, "What if the car is gone when you go back to the dealership?" Well then, it wasn't meant to be now, was it?

As a parallel to relationships: Some women will see a guy they like and start thinking how good they would look on this man's arm, which causes their emotions to start climbing. Men, just like women, know how emotions work, and The Chameleon, like the car salesman, is trained by experience to tailor his behavior to the current situation in order to get the results he desires. He will try to increase your emotions, since this will make his job of convincing you that much easier. If you step away from the situation, you can better make a rational decision you can live with without regret and actually be pleased you have made the right choice. The insecure woman, however, doesn't want to risk losing this guy, so she offers an easy path of success for him.

Your rational mind must assist you in making your decisions when the time arrives, thus placing your personal wellbeing over instant gratification.

Once you have figured out how to master your emotions instead of letting someone else do so, you will be able to enjoy any situation presented to you. The confidence of knowing you can be in any situation without having to worry about anyone playing games with your emotions allows you to let your hair down and just have fun.

If you are among friends and have too much to drink, you know you don't have to worry because your friends won't allow you to make an ass of yourself. Once you have mastered your emotions, you will be in control and can now experience this same secure feeling in any situation because you are now your own best friend—you will be looking out for *you*.

Of course, the best case scenario is someone getting another's emotions going without even trying and vice versa. If by just being yourself the other person finds you engaging or funny, you are at the ultimate starting point since you can maintain being yourself with no problem. This is also the foundation for a good friendship, which is essential in a successful relationship.

In the end, how you respond to a situation is a choice you make, so choose to control your emotions.

Chapter 6
Love and Emotion

❧❧❧

The word "love" has such a powerful effect on people that to abuse it has become commonplace in our society. Many have used love as an excuse to continue down paths of certain destruction hoping the power of love has some miraculous effect on their situations. This "love conquers all" mentality might work in a vacuum, but because of outside influences you must take responsibility for your actions. First and foremost is the fact that another person with his own issues, beliefs, and motives is involved.

If together you are not seeking the same result, there is very little love can do to help your cause. Working toward the same end result with love as your bond does not guarantee success, but it greatly increases your chances. Even failure can be accepted with more grace if love was truly involved.

If you are seeking a long-term committed relationship and he isn't, the fact that you love him will have very little effect on his decision making. If, however, you both want this committed relationship but there are issues to be worked out, being in love and both wanting the same thing makes working out the issues that much easier. It is easier to compromise with someone you love because you think he or she is worth it.

The problem some women run into is that they over-estimate the power of their love and end up thinking they have enough love for two. These women will try to convince a man that together they were meant to be and try to prove this by overcompensating. They will bend over backward, oblivious to the fact that they are doing more harm than good or that this man is just not into them.

The fact is you can't force anyone to love you. This is a path the man must see and voluntarily choose on his own. Don't try to convince a man to be with you; he must want to do so on his own, otherwise you have already lost but just don't know it yet.

For love to exist, it has to arise out of a true appreciation for that with which it is associated. Whether it is a man and his old classic car, a woman and her yoga class, or parents and their children, if you don't appreciate the meaning or existence of the object or situation there is no way you can love it.

Men know that in most cases for every dollar they invest in restoring an old car they will only get fifty cents in return if they were to sell the car. But they do the restoration anyway, because the self-gratification they get after completing such a project is priceless. The same goes for anything else where love is concerned. The effort and sacrifice required is justified by how it makes you feel in the end.

If you believe the last sentence above, then it goes to reason that if a man refuses to make compromises or sacrifices for you, *he is not in love with you!* It might seem like a harsh thing to say, but think about it before you move on.

This is not to say this man is cold and callous, because he will make sacrifices and compromises *if* he thinks it's worth it. At this moment, you might not be worth it to him. If he doesn't do these things for you, it's best to move on. Resist the urge to convince him, and don't convince yourself that you can't see yourself without him in your life. If you do either, you will end up trying to convince him until he finds someone he is willing to make sacrifices for—then he will be gone anyway.

Love, it seems, can make a normally smart person do stupid things. It is not love, however, but rather love's traveling partner that causes us to do stupid things and look foolish. Wherever love goes, there, working in the background, is…emotions!

Think for a moment about the most unemotional people you know. In their normal day-to-day lives, nothing seems to get them going. Once the situation changes to something they love, it's like a shot of adrenaline—you can't shut them up. People naturally get passionate whenever love of anything is involved, and with that passion comes emotions.

The word "love"has been abused by both men and women alike. When working on closing a deal in a relationship, whether it's for sex, emotional satisfaction, or simply trying to convince the other person to sleepover, the word "love" is thrown in the mix with the sole purpose of increasing the emotions involved. Doing this is obviously an attempt to have the other person make an emotional decision. Needless to say, for a chameleon, the word "love" is his ace in the hole—used in case of emergency.

Love is not to be taken lightly, so whenever it is introduced, serious dialogue should accompany it to eliminate the possibility of deceit. This is not the time to be blinded by love. This moment is the time to ask the tough, uncomfortable questions and not get caught up in the emotions of the moment.

How do you know if someone means it when they say they love you? Love must be proven, period. The word on its own has absolutely no value. The show of love usually involves some form of sacrifice later in the relationship, so checking the truth of someone's word is just a matter of observing his behavior in the right situations.

Whether it's cancelling or being late for a prior engagement to do something for you or going out of his way to see you, a sacrifice is the only way to prove love. If the only things that get done are those that fall within his normal daily routine, then those things do not prove love. If he has to adjust his daily routine to accommodate your request, then you are on to something.

A person must show through his or her actions the care and appreciation it takes when love is involved. If after he says he loves you a man cannot find the time to spend with you or always has an excuse why he can't do this or that, you are smart enough to know he's failing the love test. He might see you from time to time, but it won't be because of love. Don't make excuses for him, because he will make time when it's worth it to him. Again, love must be proven.

There should be no ultimatums where love is concerned, e.g., we could be together if...you lose weight, or if...you stop talking to this person, or if...the list goes on and on. Don't let anyone quantify you. They either accept you as you are or work with you on the things *you* choose to change/improve. Don't trade a good friend for a new man.

A good man will respect the fact that you need others in your life to maintain a good balance. If a man insists that you get rid of a friend, be careful, as this could be "breakdown by isolation." You could be in the company of a control freak.

If someone genuinely loves you, he must be able to allow you to be yourself and not what he wants you to be. He should be able to appreciate you for who you are and not what others think of you.

Chapter 7

The End Game

❧

Ultimately, it is all about being happy. Sometimes it might seem as if this whole dating scene is not worth the hassle it brings. However, despite all the associated frustrations, we know that finding that right person is truly worth waiting for. The key is to minimize your frustrations by continuing to live your own life even after you think you have found the right person.

Most men are not Chameleons, but because of their nature, Chameleons circulate more and leave lasting negative impressions, thus making it seem as if they are in the majority. A guy might enter a relationship with a woman then curtail it because of incompatibility, but this doesn't make him a Chameleon. A Chameleon would keep the relationship going even though he knows it is going nowhere.

This action only validates the need for a woman to allow time to get to know a potential partner. While not all situations can be covered before starting a relationship, at least get the basics out of the way. Can you both deal with each other when you are at your worst? Are you compatible beyond the physical stuff, i.e. financial, kids, friends, family, or lifestyle, etc.? Can this person be your best friend?

There is a lot involved in forming a lasting long-term relationship, and that is why allowing situations to develop over time to help you build a strong foundation is so important. Continue living your normal life as you slowly blend this new situation into the mix. Enjoy all that this new situation has to give, but be mindful not to let your emotions start making your decisions.

If the relationship is new, your emotions will be raging and you might get the feeling to "run with it." This feeling is usually caused by either insecurity or desperation. You can minimize insecurity by believing in yourself, and desperation can be eliminated by living a balanced life.

As time progresses, you must determine if your partner is as committed to a future together as you are. This can only be proven by unprompted actions on his part. If you have to keep asking how serious he is about "us," then you must re-evaluate your situation. The relationship must enhance both your lives for it to survive.

If you are currently in an ongoing relationship that started out promising, it is easy to settle with what you currently have even though you know it is not what you want. Don't let frustration or "time served" force you into settling, as this only guarantees a life of "what ifs." This is a miserable existence and a hard road to travel. If the relationship is going in a different direction than you had discussed and he has proven he is not committed to making the relationship better, you must summon the strength to move on. This is why you must know what you want and what your partner says he wants before making long-term commitments. Time, situations, and communication are your best tools.

Most relationships fail during the selection process, so select your partner wisely. To maximize your success, your partner needs to be on the same wavelength as you are and be someone who has figured "it" out. At the very least he should have a good grasp on where he wants to go and how he plans to get there. This, of course, must be on the same path as your own goals and aspirations. If your partner is still in his "boy" stage, you will be wasting your time while he tries to figure it out. Do not be influenced by others if deep down this is not what you want. What others think should have little to do with who you choose to be with. Some people will find negative things to say no matter how well you are doing, so you might as well be happy with whatever decisions you choose to make in life.

Relationships should have a natural flow. If you have to draw up a game plan in order to win this man over, there is something wrong since he should want this relationship as much as you do.

Don't be overwhelmed by the process. Find yourself before you take on the task of adding someone new to your life. Once you have accomplished the task of finding yourself, your perspective on life will be greatly changed and life itself will become that much easier.

www.ingramcontent.com/pod-product-compliance
Lightning Source LLC
Chambersburg PA
CBHW071006040426
42443CB00007B/694